Dr Ritu Arora

300 GREAT TO EAT OIL FREE RECIPES

HEALTH HARMONY

300 GREAT TO EAT OIL FREE RECIPES

First Edition: 2013
1st Impression: 2013

All rights reserved. No part of this book may be reproduced, stored in a retrieval system or transmitted, in any form or by any means, mechanical, photocopying, recording or otherwise, without any prior written permission of the publisher.

© with the author

Published by Kuldeep Jain for

HEALTH HARMONY
An imprint of
B. JAIN PUBLISHERS (P) LTD.
An ISO 9001: 2000 Certified Company
1921/10, Chuna Mandi, Paharganj, New Delhi 110 055 (INDIA)
Tel.: +91-11-4567 1000 • *Fax:* +91-11-4567 1010
Email: info@bjain.com • *Website:* **www.bjain.com**

Printed in India by
J.J. Offset Printers

ISBN: 978-81-319-1956-9

Dedication

He gives me Vision To dream & Gives me
A wonderful Team to fulfill The dreams
Thanks to everyone
Dedicated To My Parents & My family

Dr Ritu Arora

PREFACE

Roti, kapda aur makan are the three basics requirements of mankind since time immemorial.

The concept of eating started right from the day man was born. Eating owes its origin to the Stone Age when man began to eat fruits, leafy vegetables and raw meat. Gradually, with the discovery of fire, the process of cooking food evolved. As a result, new developments were seen not only in the appearance and preparation of food but also in the modes of cooking and use of condiments and spices.

Since ages the medium of cooking has been oil, ghee and butter with varying components of PUFA AND MUFA. With the advent of time, varying complex diseases have cropped up due to lifestyle and its associated changes, some due to food changes and some are genetic. But with time, awareness and concern regarding their health has also developed among people.

Oh! Doctor, I am suffering from diabetes and you have given me a long list of medicines, but how about my Diet, the type of food and so on. Look I am overweight; do guide me about my calorie intake, the type of food I should eat. All these queries are being raised by the patients and their attendants.

This book has been written keeping in mind the concerns of people regarding their health and all the possibilities available for a GOOD COOKING MEDIUM, MODE OF COOKING and DIFFERENT PRESENTATIONS OF THE COOKED FOOD.

It has been my intense desire to start a centre called NUTRIPOINT which will cater to highly balanced and nutritious OIL FREE FOOD.

This book presents more than 300 different, simple recipes which have been all practically tried and contain good nutritive value.

ACKNOWLEDGEMENT

300 Oil Free Recipes has been a dream of mine because a good balanced diet when advised by the doctor helps the patient to improve his tendency for many diseases.

This book is purely original and all the recipes and their preparations have been formulated by the author.

I started on this project when my father underwent By Pass surgery in the year 2001 (May), followed by multiple complications.

As per dietary norms, boiled food is definitely not acceptable. It was then that the IDEA OF OIL FREE COOKING with different formulations came to my mind.

All the recipes included in the book are original, formulated by the doctor and are health oriented.

I am thankful to Mr. Kuldeep Jain, M.D., B. Jain Publishing Group for supporting my work.

I am thankful to Mr. Rajan Kapoor, Mrs. Simran Mehandiratta, Mrs. Tina Kalra, and Sarthak Tikoo for making best contributions in this work.

This work is purely dedicated to my PARENTS, MY FAMILY AND MY WELL WISHERS.

May everyone reads this work and learns the ART OF OIL FREE COOKING.

EXPERT COMMENTS & COMPLIMENTS

I am 76-year-old, retired as a General Manager from India Tourism Development Corporation (Agent of India Undertaking). I was allowed free entertainment in any hotel. I am totally vegetarian, non-smoker, non-drinker, and non-diabetic.

I have been very fond of pakoras, samosas and other fried items. Potato puri has been my biggest weakness. I have not left any chat corner of Delhi. I am also very fond of choley bhature. For the last five years, Dr. Ritu has changed my eating habits. My diet is as under:

- I take stuffed parantha without oil, butter etc. and with curd and mango pickle and a glass of juice for breakfast. In lunch, I take one chapatti with one vegetable without oil or ghee and with lassi. I take curd lassi regularly throughout the year in lunch.
- I take tea at 11:30 in the morning with snacks that are totally oil free, prepared by my daughter (Dr. Ritu Arora).
- I take my dinner between 9:00 p.m. to 9:30 p.m. Dinner is very light. I take either two cheese slices, or a dosa, or one uthpam. No ghee or oil is used for the preparation of these items. These items are personally prepared by my daughter (Dr. Ritu Arora).

- I regularly go for a walk for one hour daily in the morning and in the afternoon.
- I am allowed to take food from outside once a month.
- Since, I am also part of the society; I have to attend important functions. There, I try to take less oily items as the oil free food keeps me fit everywhere.
- I get my tests done once in every three months. If there is any deficiency, I try to take more precautions regarding my diet.

With the change in my food habits my lifestyle has changed completely. I am no longer tempted to eat fried food. I am indebted to my daughter Dr. RITU ARORA for my well-being. May GOD bless her.

P.C. Arora

Father

The changeover from wheat flour based Indian breads to other grains was surprisingly tasty for the taste-buds. The oil-free food is very light on the stomach. The feeling of heaviness post meals vanished resulting in more energetic and agile body. The initial feeling of lack of satiation, owing to a shift to oil free and other grains, gave way to feeling healthy every moment.

Rajan Arora

Deputy Manager (IOC)

I am indeed very thankful to Dr. Ritu for bringing this change of diet in my food regime. This is in fact not just a change of diet; it's indeed a change of mindset and change of lifestyle; introducing an absolutely new, fresh and healthy perspective into our lives. With changing time, we need to change our cooking habits and adapt to a healthier living. I have been privileged to have tasted some of the oil free recipes of Dr. Ritu Arora, which are so innovative, wholesome and nutritious. I wonder if I could have had these from the beginning. Every family must read this book and adapt to such wonderful cooking standards.

J.K. Arora
DGM Reliance Communication

Hi. We are grateful to Dr. Ritu Arora who made our life better with her magic hands. She is a real magician as well as a great cook. We had a small get together at Dr. Ritu Arora's house on her B'day. It was a great feeling to be there. The snacks served were totally prepared by the doctor itself and were totally oil free and perfectly cooked. Can you imagine.... totally oil free and yes too much delicious, nutritious and healthy.

Harish Kumar
(Businessman)

My husband loves to have spicy food most of the time but he also enjoyed a lot the food cooked by Dr. Ritu and now he wants that type of food daily especially in his breakfast and I also love to cook as that gives really a good start of the day. I am definitely going to refer this book to my all dears and nears and I am quite sure they definitely going to love and have only this type of food. Thanks to Dr. Ritu for a wonderful change in the kitchen and we wish her all the success in life.

Simran Mehandiratta
(Medical Transcription)

I and my family is extremely thankful for your book of recipes without oil. It is a wonderful book to refer to anyone and has a vast information. The BEST part is, everything is with no oil and still delicious. It has actually created a paradigm shift that we can cook varieties without oil. These words of adoration is too less for me to express the endeavors you have done to the society with all your efforts. We are proud to be associated with you and many thanks for all your initiatives.

Meenu Trikha
(IBM manager)

Hi. If I have to post an opinion on oil free food I believe it's a myth that food with good oil and fried tastes good. I cook most of the times oil free or just with minimal oil. I believe food we eat should be high in nutritional value. Oil free is good for many reasons it makes one feel very light, one is away from health issues like gastric acidity and all good for heart. I feel superbly active when I don't take a heavy meal. I have lot of recipes for oil free food all tried and tasted from Dr. Ritu Arora first oil free cooking book but my favorite is sagp salad and the tofu dish. Friends, her recipes are just too good for people who are weight and health conscious.

Shilpa Bagga
(Businesswoman)

Cooking has been my passion. My husband underwent By Pass in the year 2004 which made me more keen towards oil free cooking. I am very fond of cooking new recipes and now even my kids enjoy them. Given a chance I would like to cater oil free food on a large scale. Thanks to Dr. Ritu Arora for suggesting oil free food.

Renu Tikoo
(Interior Designer)
Sanjay Tikoo
(Businessman)

In today's high voltage lifestyle, how can a person remain mentally fit and physically strong? The answer is very simple as suggested by Dr. Ritu Arora, a doctor, a physician, and a friend. A healthy oil free food and a little walk can change your lifestyle altogether. I wish Dr. Ritu comes up out with some book elaborating the benefits of oil free food to help the millions to enjoy a healthy and a long life.

Sudhakant Sharma & Natasha Sharma (U.K.)
(Service)

PUBLISHER'S NOTE

More than often we make bad choices regarding our health. It is only when our body starts showing signs that something is wrong, do we take control of our health. But most of the time, though we take medicines, we neglect or pay no heed to our diet. Everyday, we continue to consume foods rich in oil.

There is, however, an oil free method of cooking food which compliments our health and fitness. **Dr Ritu Arora's** book **300 Oil Free Recipes** is a beacon of hope for those who are worried about their declining health. She is a practicing Homoeopath and author of several books which are best sellers. Her recipes are simple, versatile and simply delectable. These recipes cooked in mediums other than oil make them appealing in terms of taste and presentation.

I am happy to publish Dr Ritu Arora's 300 Oil Free Recipes as it is through her endeavour that we will go one step closer to a healthier and happier lifestyle.

Kuldeep Jain
C.E.O., B. Jain Publishers (P) Ltd.

CONTENTS

Preface iv
Acknowledgement vi
Expert Comments & Compliments viii
Publisher's Note xii

PART 1
FOOD 1

PART 2
WAYS AND MEANS OF COOKING 7

PART 3
INDIGENOUS NAMES 11

PART 4
DIET AND DISEASES 13

PART 5
BEVERAGES 21

Ice cream Crush 23
Fresh Lime Soda 24
Ginger/Mint Crush 25
Cucumber Crush 26
Indian Gooseberry Drink 27

Contents xiii

Guava Drink 28

Fruity Mock Tail 29

Fruit Shakes 30

Grapes Delight 31

Cumin Water 32

Water Balls 33

Kanji 34

Lime Drink 35

Mango Pulpy Drink 36

Minty Syrup 37

Black Currants Chiller 38

Papaya Chill 39

Papaya Thandai 40

Sweet Lassi 41

Spiced Buttermilk 42

Veggy Mocktail 43

Orange Flavoured Pumpkin Drink 44

Yoghurt Mix 45

Minty Coco Lime 46

Cool, Cool Thandai 47

PART 6
SOUPS 49

Tomato Soup 51

Chickpea Soup 52

Spinach Soup 53

Corn Soup 54

Hot and Sweet Soup 55

Mixed Vegetable Soup 56

Spaghetti Soup 57

Mushroom Soup 58

Cabbage Soup 59

Groundnut Soup 60

Pumpkin and Sweet Pumpkin Soup 61

Curd and Coriander Soup 62

Coconut Soup 63

Mixed Dry Fruit Soup 64

Apple Soup 65

Rice and Barley Soup 66

Beans Soup 67

Beetroot Soup 68

French Onion Soup 69

Gazpacho 70

Green Peas Soup 71

Pulse Soup 72

Fenugreek Soup 73

Soya Soup 74

Tamarind Soup 75

PART 7
SALADS & DRESSINGS 77

Mushroom and Cabbage Salad 80

Cheese and Peas Salad 81

Fresh Green Salad	82
Carrot and Radish Salad	83
Chidwa Salad	84
Beans Salad	85
Corn Salad	86
Gramflour Salad	87
Hot and Sweet Salad	88
Topioca Salad	89
Fruit Salad	90
Mixed Sprout Salad	91
Stuffed Tomato Salad	92
Stuffed Capsicum Salad	93
Sweet 'n' Sour Salad	94
Stuffed Potato Salad	95
Bread Salad	96
Cream Salad	97
Macaroni Salad	98
Chickpea Salad	99
Potato Peas Salad	100
Minty Fruit Salad	101
Sprouted Wheat Salad	102
Sweet Lime and Cucumber Salad	103
Seasoned Papaya Salad	104
Soya Salad	105
Wheat and Chick Peas Salad	106

Black Chickpea and Tomato Salad 107

Sweet potato and Beetroot Salad 108

Mixed Pulses Salad 109

Green Salad 110

Peanut and Cucumber Salad 111

Crunchy Salad 112

PART 8
SNACKS 113

Shan-E-Bread 116

Bread Poha 117

Bread Pizza 118

Bread Rolls 119

Club sandwiches 120

Cheese Cabbage Sandwich 121

Tomato Onion Sandwich 122

Merry Go Sandwiches 123

Grilled Sandwiches 124

Toast a Taste 125

Pin Hole Sandwiches 126

Bread Pakora 127

Gramflour Pancake 128

Gramflour Rolls 129

Gramflour Bread 130

Navratan Gramflour 131

Gramflour Nuts 132

Gramflour Pakoras	133
Vegetable Upma	134
Vegetable Seekh Kabab	135
Veg. Shammi Kababs	136
Veg. Pancake	137
Veg. Noodles	138
Upma	139
Stuffed Egg Whites	140
Steamed Cabbage Rolls	141
Cutlets	142
Spicy Spinach Balls	143
Idli	144
Roasted Chickpea Brittle	145
Rice Moong Pulse Idli	146
Pancake	147
Vermicelli	148
Pepper Vermicelli	149
Pao Bhaji	150
Moong Pulse Dhokla	151
Dahi Vada	152
Burgers	153
Lemon Vermicelli	154
Dosa	155
Baked Samosa	156
Baked Puris	157
Bhel Puri	158

Chidwa 159

Canopy 160

Kachori 161

Tofu Pakoras 162

Mixed Veg Pakoras 163

Baby Corn Pakoras 164

Chatpate Corns 165

Arvi Leaf Pakora 166

Crispy Pineapple 167

PART 9
VEGETABLES 169

Potato Dum 172

Cumin with Potato 173

Garlic with Potato 174

Potato Masala 175

Potato with Fenugreek/Chenopodium/Spinach 176

Potato with Peas 177

Potato with Paneer 178

Potato with Cauliflower 179

Potato Kofta 180

Onion 181

Onion with Mushroom 182

Soya Onion 183

Onion with Capsicum 184

Tomatoes 185

Tomato Curry 186

Tomato Cheese	187
Cauliflower	188
Cauliflower with Potatoes	189
Cauliflower with Peas	190
Cauliflower Korma	191
Peas	192
Peas with Paneer	193
Peas with Cauliflower	194
Peas with Mushroom	195
Carrots	196
Carrot with Potato	197
Carrot with Peas	198
Cabbage	199
Cabbage with Peas	200
Cabbage with Mushrooms	201
Beans	202
Beans with Potato	203
Pumpkin	204
Sweet Pumpkin	205
Bitter Gourd	206
Chopped Bitter Gourd	207
Lady Finger	208
Chopped Lady Finger	209
Eggplant	210
Potato with Eggplant	211

Colocasia with Eggplant	212
Colocasia with Onions	213
Eggplant with Colocasia	214
Masala colocasia	215
Vegetable Karhi	216
Capsicum	217
Capsicum with Potato	218
Capsicum Paneer	219
Radish	220
Radish with Potato	221
Nutty Mutty Ginger	222
Floating Spring Onions	223
Sweet 'n' Sour Jugnu	224
Heeng-E-Matar	225
Malai Kofta	226
Beetroot	227
Nutty Mutty Radish	228
Lotus Stem with Cheese	229
Paneer Korma	232
Shahi Paneer	233
Haryali Paneer	234
Scrambled Paneer	235
Paneer Tikka	236
Paneer Sizzler	237
Paneer Chiller	238
Paneer with Peas	239

Paneer Spinach 240
Paneer with Cauliflower 241
Paneer with Chickpeas 242
Paneer with Lobhia 243
Roxy-Boxy Paneer 244
Paneer with Colocasia 245
Nutty Ginger Paneer 246
Shahi Korma 247
Pulses and Beans 248

PART 10
RAITAS 255

Potato Raita 257
Carrot, Spinach Raita 258
Mint Raita 259
Pumpkin Raita 260
Mixed Vegetable Raita 261
Nutty Mutty Raita 262
Fruity Raita 263
Boondi Raita 264
Tomato Raita 265
Chickpea Raita 266
Cabbage Raita 267
Eggplant Raita 268
Gourd Raita 269
Chenopodium Raita 270

PART 11
PICKLES 271

Instant Mango Pickle 273
Ginger/Chilly Pickle 274
Lemon Pickle 275
Indian Gooseberry Pickle 276
Onion Pickle 277
Pumpkin Pickle 278
Yam Pickle 279
Cucumber Pickle 280
Lady's Finger Pickle 281
Green Chilly Pickle 282
Garlic Pickle 283
Mixed Vegetable Pickle 284
Ganth Cauliflower Pickle 285
Potato Pickle 286
Carrot Pickle 287
Tamarind Pickle 288
Sweet 'n' sour Garlic 289

PART 12
DIPS 291

Coriander/Mint Dip 293
Pulses Dip 294
Dates Dip 295
Tamarind Dip 296

Corinader Dip 297

Onion Dip 298

Coconut Dip 299

Raisin Dip 300

Raw Mango Dip 301

Tomato Onion Dip 302

Indian Gooseberry Dip 303

Garlic Dip 304

Radish Dip 305

Green Chilly Dip 306

Plum Dip 307

PART 13
CEREALS 309

Broken Wheat Pongal 311

Broken Wheat Pulao 312

Dahi Bhaat 313

Hariyali Pulao 314

Mushroom Pulao 315

Khichadi 316

Lemon Rice 317

Tamarind Rice 318

Tomato Rice 319

Delicious Corn flour bread 320

PART 14
SWEET DISHES 321

Rice Pudding 323

Sago Pudding	324
Cocoa Rolls	325
Vermicelli Pudding	326
Khoya Rolls	327
Kesari Raj Bhog	328
Mango Ice Cream	329
Custard with Jelly	330
Shahi Tukra	331
Nutty Mutty	332
Fruit Crush	333
StrawBerry Phirni	334
Shrikhand	335
Modak	336
Semolina Coconut Ladoo	337
Fruit Cream	338
Coconut Pudding	339
Cardamom Fudge	340
Gramflour Ladoo	341
Carrot Pudding	342
Sweet Pulse and Rice	343
Gourd Burfi	344
Moong Pulse Halwa	345
Pulse-E-Pudding	346
Pumpkin Halwa	347
Orange Spiced	348

Stuffed Pears 349

Dates Flour 350

Gulab Jamun 351

Sweet Rice 352

Dates Pudding 353

Sponge Rasgula 354

Anjeer ki Burfi 355

Rabri Faluda...: 356

Rasmalai 357

Semolina Pudding 358

Gramflour Halwa 359

Sandesh 360

Carrot Halwa 361

Kulfi 362

Sweetened Curd 363

Apple Snowballs 364

Coco Khoya 365

Potato Halwa 366

Chocopie 367

PART 15
FEW HEALTH TIPS 369

Glossary *371*

part 1
FOOD

Food is the basic requirement of every living being. The food that we eat has different components in it including carbohydrates, proteins, fats, vitamins and minerals etc. Let's understand then what the purpose of FOOD is:

FOOD

1. It gives us energy to sustain our normal daily routine which includes breathing, excretion, walking, growth and tissue repair.
2. It promotes the growth and development of the body.
3. It is the way to DIVERT YOUR STRAIN. It works as a wonderful STRESS BUSTER. That's why we tend to eat more during stress.
4. It improves the IMMUNITY of the body, thus helping the body in FIGHTING THE DISEASES.
5. It helps to SUSTAIN THE PURPOSEFUL LIVING of body.

COMPONENTS OF FOOD

The food that we eat has different basic components. Let's study them briefly to understand the importance of each and every component of what we eat.

CARBOHYDRATES

They are the simplest component of food. They can be in the form of simple sugars to complex starches. They help in building the body and also PROVIDE STRENGTH TO THE BODY.

Sources of carbohydrates: All cereals including wheat, maize, barley, rice, millets and Bengal gram; potatoes and sweet potatoes; all fresh fruits like grapes, dates and raisins have lots of carbohydrates.

PROTEINS

The body building component in food is PROTEIN which helps in HEALING THE TISSUES and in QUICK METABOLISM.

Sources: It is found in legumes and pulses: Bengal gram, lentils, curd and soya. Milk products like curd, paneer, custard also contain proteins. Meat products like chicken, fish and red meat carry lots of high animal protein. Nuts like cashew, coconut are good sources of proteins.

FATS

The oily, greasy part of food is LIPIDS/FATS. They are of 2 types: SATURATED AND UNSATURATED. The unsaturated fats are usually seen in the form of oils, thin, in low density, less voluminous. The SATURATED fats are thick and greasy. These include ghee, cream and butter.

Sources: Ghee, butter, oils (olive oil, mustard, groundnut) etc.; dry fruits like almonds, walnuts and cashews etc.; milk and milk products; meat and meat products.

VITAMINS

These are the most essential among the food components. They are beneficial in building the RESISTANCE of the body. Vitamins are of 2 types: Oil Soluble and Water Soluble.

OIL SOLUBLE VITAMINS

VITAMIN A: It is also called FAT VITAMIN. It is essential and useful for skin, bones and heart.

Sources: Green leafy vegetables like methi, spinach, sarson, chenopodium, carrots and petha. Oils like Cod liver oil, Shark liver oil, almond oil, butter, fresh cream etc. Non-vegetarian foods like fish and meat are also sources of vitamin A.

VITAMIN D: It is an essential vitamin for bone growth and development. It is an essential part of skin and bones.

SOURCES: Milk and milk products, sun exposure, oil, ghee and butter.

VITAMIN E: It is essential for a good immune system. It is very rare to get it through diet except through green vegetables and cotton seeds.

VITAMIN K: It is essentially required for bleeding control mechanism. It is found in wheat gram oil, aloe vera and wheat gram.

WATER SOLUBLE VITAMINS

These vitamins are highly sensitive to heat, light and cooking. They are soluble in water and are easily destroyed by heat and cooking. They cannot be maintained and stored for a long time.

VITAMIN B: It is an essential vitamin meant for developing RESISTANCE of the body, good skin, gums and bones.

Sources: All green vegetables, sprouts; all soya products; fortified yeast and yeast products; and soaked nuts.

VITAMIN C: The common ASCORBIC ACID is essentially a water soluble vitamin which is useful for a good skin, dental hygiene and bones of the body along with developing immunity and disease fighting power.

Sources: Sprouts; all citrus fruits like pineapple, oranges and amla etc are rich sources. Top portion of carrot is one of the most important sources of Vitamin C. Amarnath and celery leaves have plenty of ascorbic acid.

VITAMIN B12: A Very valuable vitamin which is essential for IRON ABSORPTION. It is an elementary part of Iron.

Sources: Whole milk, milk products, cheese, soybean and leafy vegetables.

FOLIC ACID

When combined with Vitamin B12, it works as a wonderful coal (a medium of energy) for the ACTIVITY OF NERVES. Deficiency of folic acid can lead to NEURITIS where TINGLING and NUMBNESS of hands and feet are the primary symptoms.

MINERALS

One of the most important components of food are minerals which include calcium, iron, phosphorus, zinc, iodine, potassium, chloride, copper and magnesium etc. Let's have a look at the body minerals.

CALCIUM

The most important component of bones and teeth is Calcium. It is seen in the form of Calcium oxalate and Calcium phosphate.

SOURCES: Milk and milk products, soybean, cheese and paneer; turnip, carrot and radish; pulses like Rajma, Lobhia and lentils are a good source of Calcium. Peanuts are a wonderful source of calcium.

PHOSPHORUS

One of the most elementary components of bones is found in milk and milk products. Cereals like oats and barley are a good source of Phosphorus.

IRON

An essential component of blood is iron which is found in green leafy vegetables like fenugreek, spinach, celery leaves. Cooking in iron utensils helps in adding iron to our diet. Non-vegetarian products like mutton, eggs and liver are good sources of iron.

IODINE

Iodine, the essential component of THYROID GLAND and required for good functioning of thyroid activity, IQ for good intelligence, is found in IODISED SALT and leafy vegetables.

ROUGHAGE AND FIBRE

The most important part of the diet which adds bulk to the food is roughage. It helps to absorb nutrients and improves intestinal mobility, enhances absorption of ESSENTIAL NUTRIENTS.

All leafy vegetables, nuts, salads, fruits like papaya, pineapple are wonderful sources of FIBRE in a diet. A GOOD FIBRE DIET WORKS LIKE WONDER FOR A GOOD HEALTH.

part 2
WAYS AND MEANS OF COOKING

Cooking is not just an ART but an ARTISTIC way to present ONE'S EMOTION, ONE'S WAY TO EXPRESS in a MODIFIED WAY.

Cooking not just aims at cooking food but also at using maximum tools with maximum results in terms of presentation, taste and temptation. There are different modes of Cooking. Let's have a look at different MODUS being used primarily in OIL FREE COOKING.

1. A NON STICK ROUND BOTTOMED PLATTER: It is primarily a medium sized round based utensil with deep ½ inch cups which are simply greased and filled up with different fillings.
2. A NON STICK PAN: Usually used for Pancakes, bread platter, pakoras and dosas.
3. INDIAN BREAD MAKER: It is a wonderful tool used for dosas, uttapam and Indian bread which is purely oil free.

DIFFERENT WAYS OF COOKING

Let's have a look at the different ways of cooking food.

1. **FRYING:** This uses oil as a medium to cook. It is of 2 types: shallow and deep.
2. **BOILING:** It is a way to cook food where the medium to cook food is water at boiling temperature of more than 100°F. It immediately destroys all the important NUTRIENTS. Very few people relish this mode of cooking.
3. **STEAMING:** It is a way of cooking food by using steam. It is an INDIRECT WAY OF COOKING. Since it is a slow process, it does not kill the NUTRIENTS. The food is light and nutritious.

4. **PARBOILING:** It is a modified way of cooking which uses the combination of steam and boiling. It is used PRIMARILY FOR BROWN RICE. It is essentially a way to RESTORE the NUTRIENTS of cooked foods.

MEDIUM USED FOR COOKING

The base used for cooking is called MEDIUM. The mediums used are:

1. Oil
2. Water
3. Milk
4. Curd

Few Principles of Cooking

1. Cook on slow flame.
2. Keep the lid covered while cooking. It saves almost 50% of the food nutrients.
3. Do not use too many condiments and spices.
4. Use cooker (steam) to the maximum for cooking to save fuel and nutrients in food.
5. Do not use salt when the food is cooked.
6. Use only BLACK SALT in food ADDITIVES like pickles and Dips.
7. Use minimum quantity of water while cooking to avoid NUTRIENTS wastage.
8. Use BEST OF COMBINATIONS to give maximum NUTRITIVE VALUE for FOOD.

part 3
INDIGENOUS NAMES

Let us have a look at the common indigenous names of some of the commonest veg./spices; condiments used in the Indian kitchen.

Cumin	(Jeera)
Asafetida	(Heeng)
Fenugreek	(Kasoori Methi)
Turmeric	(Haldi)
Black Pepper	(Kali Mirch)
Coriander	(Coriander)
Chilly Red	(Desi Mirchi)
Cloves	(Lounge)
Salt	(Namak)
Cardamom	(Elaichi)
Garlic	(Lehsun)
Tamarind	(Imli)
Mango Powder	(Amchur)
Ginger	(Adrak)
Poppy	(Postodana)
Sesame Seeds	(Til)
Charoli	(Chironji)
Jack Fruit	(Kathal)
Golden Raisins	(Kishmish)
Black Currants	(Munakka)
Semolina	(Semolina)
Cow Pea	(Black eyed beans)
Areca Nut	(Supari)

part 4
DIET AND DISEASES

DIET IN DIABETES

1. Avoid refined sugar, carbohydrates and complex starches. Honey is a good substitute for sugar.
2. Take easily digestible and palatable carbohydrates of simple origin. Rice and potatoes can be consumed in moderate amounts without fear of increasing blood sugar levels.
3. Do not keep your stomach empty for long.
4. Have a platter of salad before every meal.
5. Avoid refined foods like cake, pastries and pizzas.
6. Avoid milk at night.
7. Include more whole grain cereals and sprouts in your diet.
8. Take fenugreek seeds or Indian gooseberry powder (1/4 tsp) with honey early each morning. It reduces blood sugar levels.
9. Zamun (Jambolinum) seeds when crushed and taken with water helps in bringing down the levels of sugar.
10. Go for regular brisk walk and skipping.

DIET IN HYPERTENSION

1. Avoid table salt, oily and fried food.
2. Have 6-8 almonds and 2-3 soaked walnuts daily.
3. 1 slice of garlic every morning on empty stomach is excellent.
4. Drink plenty of water.
5. Try to take dinner either before or around 8:00 pm.
6. Flax seeds ½ teaspoon in the morning is highly beneficial.

DIET IN JOINT PAIN AND ARTHRITIS

1. Avoid pulses and cabbage. Whole grains like lentils and beans are allowed.
2. Take plenty of citrus fruits in your diet.
3. Avoid eating late and take no milk at night.
4. 5-6 drops of almond oil in 2-3 teaspoons of water is highly useful.
5. Take your meals preferably around 7:30 to 8:00 pm.
6. Cereals like maize, barley and gram flour are more beneficial than wheat.
7. Rice should be a cereal of choice rather than wheat.

RENAL / KIDNEY DIET

1. If there is a history of renal/ureteric stones, drink plenty of water. If there is a history of (H/o) nephrotic syndrome or glomerulonephritis (renal infection/renal failure) avoid overloading. Do not exceed in drinking water beyond 1.5 litres.
2. Restriction on salt and extra potassium in the form of citrus fruits should be avoided.
3. Take no leafy vegetables.
4. Fruits like papaya are not good.
5. The intake of proteins should not exceed beyond 1gm/kg body weight.
6. Red meat and eggs should be avoided.

DIET IN CARDIAC /HEART DISEASES

1. Choose the lightest and best cooking medium so that life becomes more comfortable.
2. Drink plenty of water except if LVEF (Left Ventricular Ejection Fraction) is low and cardiac monitoring is erratic.
3. Take your meals maximum by 8:00 pm.
4. Rich foods like cream, ghee, butter and ice creams should be avoided. Foods such as nuts, chocolates, malt, cold drinks should be avoided.
5. Table salt should be avoided. On the contrary do not use medicated or LONA (low sodium) salt.
6. The nuts if soaked for 12-14 hrs can be consumed easily by the cardiac patients as it changes the calorific value and fats of nuts.

DIET IN ALLERGIES

1. Avoid the intake of allergens.
2. Drink plenty of water.
3. Have good citrus fruits like amla, guava, lime and sweet lime etc. ½ to 1 lemon taken orally improves body's stamina.
4. Avoid milk especially at night.

GASTRIC DIET

A gastric may vary from being simple dyspepsia to violent aggression or Oesophagitis to Oesophageal ulcers.

1. Avoid late night watching and eating.

2. Take plenty of water.
3. Avoid pulses, cabbage and leafy vegetables.
4. Eating more of rice is beneficial.
5. Do not keep your stomach empty for long.
6. Intake of spices should be kept to a minimum.
7. Soak 5-6 pieces of raisins in ½ cup of water overnight. Take this water in the morning, and soaked kishmish after dinner to be consumed in the morning.
8. Avoid citrus fruits in hyperacidity.
9. Isabgol husk ½ teaspoon in ½ cup of water before any 2 meals of the day.

DIET IN DIARRHOEA

Diarrhoea if due to infection can primarily be controlled with diet and minimum medicines. Let's have a look.

1. Take ½ teaspoon of Glucon-D and electral powder directly on the tongue.
2. Avoid lime water and citrus juices.
3. Take no cereals for 2 days, only light biscuits or white bread can be taken.
4. Boiled potatoes are of immense use.
5. From 2nd day onwards start eating boiled rice or khichdi with fresh curd.
6. Avoid eating wheat and cereals for at least 3-4 days.
7. Do not take roughage and salads in diarrhoea.
8. Eating banana helps to improve the circulation.

DIET IN CONSTIPATION

1. Sluggishness of intestines is constipation. The causes of constipation vary from simple outer reasons to deep varied reasons and it can be due to diet and daily routine. Mood variations may also be seen.
2. Take plenty of water and fruits.
3. Roughage in the form of salads and fruits especially watermelon and pineapple are of immense importance.
4. Kishmish 5-6 pieces when soaked in water overnight has a good role to improve B.M.R (Basal Metabolic Rate).
5. Take castor oil (5-10) drops with tea leaves after the leaves have been put in boiled water. It has major impact on constipation.
6. Avoid eating full meals, have 5-6 broken meals.

DIET IN SKIN DISEASES

1. Take plenty of water.
2. Additives, preservatives and synthetic foods should be avoided as much as possible.
3. Take citrus fruits in plenty.
4. Avoid irritating foods like vinegar; also avoid spicy food.

DIET IN RESPIRATORY DISEASES

1. Avoid milk. However, milk products can be taken comfortably even in the evening and at night also.

2. Put 1 drop of almond oil in both nostrils at night.
3. Take early dinner and a short nap can be refreshing also.
4. Take camphor steam 1-2 times a day.

DIET IN OBESITY

1. Calculate your calories and maintain your caloric balance.
2. Take plenty of water and do regular exercises.
3. Avoid oily, high carbohydrates, high fat foods.
4. Take small foods (snacks) like chidwa (beaten rice with pea nuts), roasted seeds, and popcorns in between meals instead of heavy meals.
5. Depend more on green leafy vegetables and salads.
6. Avoid at least one cereal meal a day.
7. Consume toned milk.
8. Depend on limited food combinations.
9. Do not eat a variety of foods as it increases the appetite and thus the weight.
10. Warm water with ½ teaspoon lemon juice and ¼ teaspoon honey is a good stimulant for fat reduction.
11. Sipping warm water in phases helps to overcome this modified stored fat.

DIET IN THYROID DISORDERS

Avoid cabbage when hypothyroidism prevails.

DIET IN UNDER NUTRITION

1. Consume high protein foods like milk, milk products, legumes, beans etc.
2. Take moderate proteins and good carbohydrates.
3. Full cream milk should be taken.

DIET IN FEVERS

1. Consume large quantities of water.
2. Avoid taking stimulants.
3. In gastroenteritis, glucose water, electoral and lemon water should be given.
4. Take more carbohydrates and less fats.
5. In Hepatitis; low fat, high carbohydrate foods such as rice, khichri, fruits, tined skimmed milk should be consumed.
6. Glucose water should be consumed in plenty.
7. In typhoid, avoid fats, take more carbohydrates, moderate proteins and water.
8. In virals, do not stop eating. Keep eating frequently.
9. In U.T.I (urinary tract infections) take splenty of fluids, more of alkaline foods and liquids.

part 5
BEVERAGES

This is one of the most important and the most neglected area in cooking especially in the Indian scenario. It plays a very important role especially for those patients who have to be dependent more on a semisolid diet. The beverages used contain minimum calories and are highly nutritious in terms of Vitamin C and a few even have Calcium in them.

Let us understand few recipes of common beverages.

- Ice-cream Crush
- Fresh Lime Soda
- Ginger/Mint Crush
- Cucumber Crush
- Indian Gooseberry Drink (Amla)
- Guava Drink
- Fruity Mock Tail
- Fruit Shakes
- Cumin Water
- Water Balls
- Kanji
- Lime Drink
- Mango Pana
- Minty Syrup
- Black Currants Chiller (Munakka)
- Papaya Chill
- Papaya Thandai
- Sweet Lassi
- Spiced Butter Milk
- Veggy Mock Tail
- Orange Flavoured Pumpkin Drink
- Yoghurt Mix
- Minty Coco Lime
- Cool Cool Thandai

ICE CREAM CRUSH

INGREDIENTS

1. Vanilla ice-cream — 1 cup
2. Orange squash — 4 tsp
3. Soda water — 1

METHOD

(1) Mix soda water with orange squash. Put it in a mixer and churn it.

(2) Add vanilla ice-cream and again churn it in the mixer.

(3) Serve chilled.

FRESH LIME SODA

INGREDIENTS

1. Lemon juice — 2 tsp
2. Soda water — 200 ml
3. Sugar — 2 tsp
4. Black salt — To taste
5. Sliced sweet lime (Mosambi) — 1

METHOD

(1) Mix lemon juice, sugar and black salt.//
(2) Add chilled soda water.
(3) Garnish with sliced sweet lime and serve chilled.

GINGER/MINT CRUSH

INGREDIENTS

1.	Ginger (crushed)	1 tsp
2.	Mint leaves (crushed)	10-15
3.	Soda water	200 ml
4.	Black salt	Pinch
5.	Cumin powder	Pinch
6.	Black pepper	Pinch

METHOD

(1) Crush ginger and mint separately.

(2) Mix crushed ginger and mint. Add soda water.

(3) Churn them in the mixer.

(4) Serve chilled with added taste of black pepper, black salt, and cumin powder.

CUCUMBER CRUSH

INGREDIENTS

1.	Cucumber (fresh; medium size)	2
2.	Coconut (grated)	30-40 g
3.	Milk toned	½ cup
4.	Sugar	1 tsp
5.	Salt black and black pepper	To taste

METHOD

(1) Peel the skin of cucumber and grate it. Mix it with grated coconut.

(2) Put cucumber, coconut and toned milk in the mixer, blend it thoroughly.

(3) Then, keep it on low flame; till it becomes thick. Let it cool. Add sugar, black pepper and salt.

(4) Serve chilled.

INDIAN GOOSEBERRY DRINK

INGREDIENTS

1. Indian Gooseberry fresh
   (if not dry Indian Gooseberry)　　　　　2-3
2. Cumin powder (roasted)　　　　　½ tsp
3. Black salt　　　　　To taste
4. Sugar　　　　　To taste
5. Mint leaves (finely chopped)　　　　　A few

METHOD

(1) Soak dry Indian Gooseberry for 1-1½ hours in a litre of water.

(2) If you are using fresh Indian Gooseberry, wash them thoroughly. Soak it in water for 2-3 hours. Bring it to a boil.

(3) When it becomes thick, add sugar, salt, and cumin powder.

(4) Blend this mixture in the mixer and serve chilled, decorated with mint leaves.

GUAVA DRINK

INGREDIENTS

1. Guavas (medium size) fresh ripe   ½ kg (5-6)
2. Sugar   4-5 tsp
3. Glacial acetic acid   1 tsp
4. Pineapple and guava   2 slices

METHOD

(1) Cut pineapple and guava into small pieces.

(2) Mix it with water and blend it in the mixer, add sugar and strain it through a fine sieve.

(3) Bring it to heat on low flame, till it becomes thick.

(4) When cool, add glacial acetic acid.

(5) Serve chilled.

FRUITY MOCK TAIL

INGREDIENTS

1.	Black tea	½ cup
2.	Lemon juice	1 tsp
3.	Orange juice	½ cup
4.	Pineapple juice	½ cup
5.	Sugar	4 tsp
6.	Ginger	1 small piece
7.	Water (for ginger extract)	½ cup
8.	Mint leaves	A few
9.	Lemon slices	2
10.	Soda	¼ bottle

METHOD

(1) Mix cold strained tea with the fruit juices.

(2) Stir in sugar and chill.

(3) For ginger extract, crush small ginger pieces and boil with ½ cup of water for 10 minutes. Strain and cool.

(4) Mix ginger extract with the juice mixture.

(5) Pour over crushed ice and serve in glasses garnished with mint leaves and lemon slices.

(6) Add soda before serving to make the taste more aromatic.

FRUIT SHAKES

INGREDIENTS

1.	Milk toned and cool	200 ml
2.	Any seasonal fruit (Chikoo/apple/banana/mango)	1
3.	Vanilla essence	¼ tsp
4.	Cinnamon powder	Pinch
5.	Ice cubes	crushed

METHOD

(1) Peel and slice the fruit to be used into small pieces.

(2) Blend it in the mixer. Add milk and vanilla essence.

(3) Put ice cubes and blend it gently.

(4) Serve cool with cinnamon powder.

NOTE: To give it a better taste, according to the fruits used, different essences like vanilla or strawberry or chocolate can be used.

GRAPES DELIGHT

INGREDIENTS

1. Black grapes — 1 cup
2. Honey — 2 tsp
3. Curd — ½ cup

METHOD

(1) Wash grapes thoroughly and put them in the mixer.

(2) Add honey and curd.

(3) Blend the mixture and then sieve the mixture.

(4) Serve chilled.

CUMIN WATER

INGREDIENTS

1.	Tamarind juice (water)	½ cup
2.	Lemon juice	2 tsp
3.	Salt	To taste
4.	Black salt	¼ tsp
5.	Cumin powder (roasted)	¼ tsp
6.	Black cumin powder	Pinch
7.	Cloves	2-3
8.	Garam masala	Pinch
9.	Mint leaves	A few
10.	Coriander leaves	A few
11.	Green chillies	2

METHOD

(1) Soak tamarind in a cup of water for ½ hour. Strain the water and tamarind juice is ready to use.
(2) Take a jug and fill it with water.
(3) Add lemon juice, tamarind juice, salt, black salt, garam masala, and powdered cumin.
(4) Blend black pepper and cloves and reduce them to a powder.
(5) Wash mint, coriander leaves and chillies together. Blend them into a mixture.
(6) Mix them well in the container.
(7) Mix all components and serve chilled.

Note: Garam Masala: corinander seeds, cumin seeds, black pepper corns, black cumin seeds, dry ginger powder, cardamom, cloves, cinnamon.

WATER BALLS

INGREDIENTS

1. Pulse Urad (soaked for balls)	½ cup
2. Soda bicarbonate	Pinch
3. Salt	To taste

FOR WATER

Cumin water powder or cumin water prepared as per details:

1. Lemon juice	1 tsp
2. Black salt	¼ tsp
3. Water	½ litre

METHOD

(1) Soak urad pulse overnight with a pinch of soda bicarbonate and salt.
(2) Blend it in a mixer and make a paste.
(3) Stir it thoroughly with a spoon so that it becomes thick.
(4) Take a glass plate and make small round balls of the mixture. Put the balls on the plate and heat them in the microwave for 1-3 minutes.
(5) Take these balls and soak them in warm water for 5-10 minutes.
(6) Press the balls between the slices of newspaper, so that the extra water is drained over.
(7) Mix cumin water powder, black salt and lemon juice in water and stir the mixture well.
(8) Mix these balls and serve cool.

KANJI

INGREDIENTS

1. Red carrots — 5-6
2. Salt — 1 tsp
3. Water — 1 litre
4. Black salt — ¼ tsp
5. Black cumin — ¼ tsp
6. Mustard seeds (powdered) — 50 g
7. Red chilly dry — 1

METHOD

(1) Wash the carrots thoroughly and cut them into pieces.

(2) Take water in a glass container and add carrots, salt, black cumin, mustard powder and red chilly to it.

(3) Stir the mixture well.

(4) Keep it in sun for 5-6 days.

(5) Serve chilled/cool.

LIME DRINK

INGREDIENTS

1. Rose syrup — 1 tsp
2. Lemon juice — 2 tsp
3. Ginger juice — ½ tsp
4. Sweet lime juice — 2 cups
5. Crushed ice

METHOD

(1) Mix all the ingredients well.
(2) Serve cool with crushed ice.

MANGO PULPY DRINK

INGREDIENTS

1.	Mangoes raw	2-3
2.	Sugar	100 gm
3.	Mint leaves dry	Few
4.	Salt	To taste
5.	Black salt	To taste
6.	Cumin powder	To taste

METHOD

(1) Wash the mangoes and pressure cook them in the cooker till they become soft.

(2) Remove the peel and separate the pulp from the mango seed.

(3) Mix sugar, black salt and cumin powder to the pulp.

(4) Cook it on low flame.

(5) Allow it to cool.

(6) Serve it cool, garnished with mint leaves.

MINTY SYRUP

INGREDIENTS

1. Mint solution — 2 tsp
2. Pineapple juice — 1 tsp
3. Cola syrup/flavour — 2 tsp
4. Lemon — 1 slice
5. Mint syrup — 1 tsp
6. Cherry — 1

METHOD

(1) Pour mint syrup in a glass.

(2) Add pineapple juice and cola flavour to it.

(3) Add crushed ice without disturbing the layers.

(4) Garnish it with lemon juice, mint leaves and cherry.

BLACK CURRANTS CHILLER

INGREDIENTS

1.	Black currants (munakka)	1 cup soaked
2.	Black salt	1 tsp
3.	Cumin powder (roasted)	½ tsp
4.	Cinnamon powder	½ tsp
5.	Sugar	4 tsp
6.	Lemon slice & mint sprig to garnish	4

METHOD

(1) Make a paste of soaked Black currants.

(2) To this paste add sugar, rest of the ingredients and mix them well.

(3) Add 2 glasses of water and mix again.

(4) Put the mixture into glasses and serve chilled.

PAPAYA CHILL

INGREDIENTS

1. Papaya (ripe, peeled & chopped into pieces) — 2 large
2. Lemon juice — ½ lemon
3. Sugar syrup — 1½ cups
4. Water — 2½ cups
5. Sugar — 2 cups

METHOD

(1) In a blender or food processor, puree papaya and add lemon juice to it.

(2) Stir in the sugar syrup and place in an aluminum pan and freeze it.

(3) Place this frozen puree again in the blender and blend it till it becomes fluffy.

(4) Transfer it to a plastic container and freeze for at least an hour before serving.

PAPAYA THANDAI

INGREDIENTS

1. Papaya (cut into pieces) — Small size
2. Orange — 1
3. Lemon — 1
4. Mint — 1 sprig
5. Sugar — 2 tsp
6. Black salt — ¼ tsp

METHOD

(1) Peel and separate the segments of orange.

(2) Mix them together with papaya, lemon juice, sugar, salt and them blend it with crushed ice.

(3) Put the mixture into glasses and garnish it with mint leaves.

(4) Serve chilled.

SWEET LASSI

INGREDIENTS

1. Curd (skimmed milk) — 1 cup
2. Sugar (powder) — 2 tsp
3. Cardamom powder — ½ tsp
4. Vanilla essence — ¼ tsp
5. Ice cubes — Crushed
6. Water — 1 cup

METHOD

(1) Churn curd thoroughly and mix it in the blender with adequate water so that it is thick.

(2) Mix it well in the blender.

(3) Add sugar, vanilla essence and ice. Mix it well.

(4) Serve chilled, garnished with cardamom powder.

SPICED BUTTERMILK

INGREDIENTS

1.	Curd (skimmed milk)	1 cup
2.	Curry leaves	A few
3.	Red chilly (whole)	1
4.	Coriander leaves (chopped)	1 tsp
5.	Mustard seeds	¼ tsp
6.	Salt	To taste

METHOD

1. Beat the curd with 2 cups of water, salt and red chilly.
2. Heat a pan and add mustard seeds. When they splutter, add coriander leaves, red chilly and pour over chilled butter milk to it. Chill it further.
3. Pour the mixture into glasses garnished with coriander leaves.

VEGGY MOCKTAIL

INGREDIENTS

1. Tomatoes (medium size, ripe) — 2
2. Carrot — 1
3. Beetroot — 1 sprig
4. Mint leaves — 1 sprig
5. Coriander leaves — 1 sprig
6. Salt — ½ tsp
7. Black salt — ¼ tsp
8. Black pepper powder — ¼ tsp
9. Cumin powder (roasted) — ¼ tsp

METHOD

(1) Wash all the vegetables thoroughly.
(2) Juice out the tomatoes, carrots, beetroot, mint and coriander leaves.
(3) Add salt and mix them well.
(4) Put the mixture into glasses and garnish it with pepper powder, black salt and roasted cumin.
(5) Serve it chilled.

ORANGE FLAVOURED PUMPKIN DRINK

INGREDIENTS

1.	Carrots (medium size)	3
2.	Red pumpkin	500 gm
3.	Onion (medium size)	1
4.	Green chillies	2
5.	Cumin seeds	1 tsp
6.	Fresh coriander leaves	A few
7.	Salt	To taste
8.	Orange juice (fresh)	1 cup
9.	Curd or low fat cream	½ cup

METHOD

(1) Wash, peel and roughly chop carrots. Peel, remove seeds of red pumpkin and roughly chop into pieces. Peel and roughly chop onion. Wash, remove stems and chop green chillies.

(2) Dry roast cumin seeds, cool and ground them to a fine powder. Clean, wash and pat dry fresh coriander leaves.

(3) Heat a sauce pan, add chopped carrots, red pumpkin, onion, green chilies and one cup water. Cook on medium heat for 8-10 minutes or till the vegetables are soft.

(4) Cool the cooked vegetables slightly and make a puree in the blender.

(5) Add roasted cumin powder, salt and one cup water to the vegetables puree and bring it to a boil. Reduce heat, add fresh orange juice and simmer for 2-3 minutes.

(6) Stir in the fresh cream and serve hot, garnished with fresh coriander leaves.

YOGHURT MIX

INGREDIENTS

1.	Carrots (medium size)	1
2.	French beans	4-6
3.	Capsicum (medium size)	1
4.	Cauliflower (small)	5-6
5.	Ginger	1
6.	Green chillies	2
7.	Yoghurt	1 cup
8.	Gramflour	2 tsp
9.	Sugar	¼ tsp
10.	Salt	To taste
11.	Milk	2 tsp
12.	Cumin seeds	1 tsp
13.	Green beans	2 tsp

METHOD

(1) Wash, peel and chop carrots, fresh beans, capsicum and cauliflower florets.
(2) Wash and chop green chillies, ginger, and grind them to a fine paste.
(3) Whisk yoghurt with 3 cups of water. Add gramflour, ginger, chilly paste, sugar and salt and blend them well.
(4) Heat milk in a pan; add cumin seeds to it and stir till it becomes brown. Add chopped vegetables and stir well till they becomes soft.
(5) Stir in the yoghurt mixture. Bring it to a boil, reduce heat and simmer for 8-10 minutes till it becomes thick.
(6) Serve hot.

MINTY COCO LIME

INGREDIENTS

1. Coconut water (fresh) — 1
2. Lemon juice — 2 tsp
3. Mint leaves (crushed) — Few
4. Sugar — ¼ tsp
5. Cumin powder — Pinch
6. Garam masala — Pinch

METHOD

(1) Freeze coconut water.

(2) Mix lemon juice, sugar and mint leaves.

(3) Take coconut water out of the chiller and mix all the ingredients (lemon juice, sugar and mint leaves).

(4) Blend it well in the mixer and serve chilled with cumin and garam masala on top.

Note: Garam Masala: corinander seeds, cumin seeds, black pepper corns, black cumin seeds, dry ginger powder, cardamom, cloves, cinnamon.

COOL, COOL THANDAI

INGREDIENTS

1.	Milk toned (chilled)	2 cup
2.	Melon seeds	100 gm
3.	Sugar (powder)	3 tsp
4.	Cardamom powder (Elaichi)	1 tsp
5.	Corn flour	2 tsp
6.	Pistachio powder	2 tsp
7.	Almond powder	2 tsp

METHOD

(1) Soak melon seeds in 1 cup of water for 2-3 hours.

(2) Blend this mixture in a blender and add corn flour, sugar, cardamom powder, pistachio and almond powder.

(3) Now add the remaining milk and serve chilled.

part 6
SOUPS

Soups are one of the basic components of Thai, Continental and Chinese food values. But with the passage of time, it has become a part of Indian tables also. Though the tradition of taking and serving soups has been quite old but by giving it a fine shape of food values has made it an important part of our food. In today's mechanical world, people find no time to prepare and serve soup; that is why all ready-made ketchups are being marketed. These have preservatives added to them.

Let us try some of the common and easily available home made soups which are easy to prepare and are nutritious also.

- Tomato Soup
- Chickpea Soup
- Spinach Soup
- Corn Soup
- Hot and Sweet Soup
- Mixed Veg. Soup
- Spaghetti Soup
- Mushroom Soup
- Cabbage Soup
- Ground Nut Soup
- Pumpkin and Sweet Pumpkin Soup
- Curd and Coriander Soup
- Coconut Soup
- Mixed Dry Fruit Soup
- Apple Soup
- Rice and Barley Soup
- Beans Soup
- Beetroot Soup
- French Onion Soup
- Gazpacho Soup
- Green Peas Soup
- Pulse Soup
- Fenugreek Soup
- Soya Soup
- Tamarind Soup

TOMATO SOUP

INGREDIENTS

1.	Tomatoes (fresh, ripe)	500 gm
2.	Sugar	2 tsp
3.	Salt and Black pepper	¼ tsp each
4.	Milk	50 ml
5.	Corn Flour	2 tsp
6.	Cloves	5-6
7.	Carrots	2
8.	Potatoes (Raw or boiled medium)	1

METHOD

(1) Wash potatoes, carrots and tomatoes. Cut them into small pieces altogether. Add cloves, sugar and salt to them.

(2) Put then in a pressure cooker and cook for 10-12 min. Let it cool.

(3) Strain the mixture and keep the pulp aside. Put the remaining pulp to water. Churn it in the mixer.

(4) Strain again and mix it with the soup.

(5) Keep it on a low flame. Allow it to boil, till it thickens up.

(6) Mix milk and corn flour. Warm it slightly. Add it to the soup and serve hot with a sandwich or pasta.

CHICKPEA SOUP

INGREDIENTS

1. Black Chickpea + white chickpea — 200 gm (100 gm each)
2. Salt, black pepper (powder) — ¼ tsp, ¾ tsp
3. Cumin powder — ½ tsp
4. Cloves — 2-3
5. Grated cheese (processed) — 10-15 gm

METHOD

(1) Wash Chickpea and soak it overnight.

(2) Bring it to boil for 10-15 min.

(3) Strain the fluid. Keep it on flame and add cumin powder, black pepper, salt and cloves. Boil it till the mixture thickens.

(4) Serve hot with garnished, processed cheese.

SPINACH SOUP

INGREDIENTS

1.	Spinach	500 gm
2.	Carrot (medium)	2
3.	Garam Masala	To taste
4.	Salt	¼ tsp
5.	Onion (chopped small)	1
6.	Lemon Juice	2 tsp

METHOD

(1) Wash spinach. Chop carrot finely. Mix them together and steam cook them in a pressure cooker for 10 min.

(2) Strain the fluid. Beat the soft boiled spinach and make a thin paste.

(3) Put few drops of lemon juice in a pan, heat it for 2-3 min. Add chopped onions and allow them to turn brown. Mix the spinach paste. Allow it to boil for 5-7 min. Add garam masala and salt to the mixture.

(4) Serve hot.

Note: Garam Masala: corinander seeds, cumin seeds, black pepper corns, black cumin seeds, dry ginger powder, cardamom, cloves, cinnamon.

CORN SOUP

INGREDIENTS

1.	Corns (boiled)	200 gm
2.	Tomatoes (medium size)	2-3
3.	Sugar	2-3 tsp
4.	Salt and garam masala	¼ tsp each
5.	Corn flour	2 tsp

METHOD

(1) Boil Tomatoes. Reduce them to a pulp. Mix corn flour and make a paste.

(2) Steam boil corns. Add tomato pulp, sugar, salt and garam masala to it. Bring it to boil. Allow it to become thick.

(3) Serve hot.

Note: Garam Masala: corinander seeds, cumin seeds, black pepper corns, black cumin seeds, dry ginger powder, cardamom, cloves, cinnamon.

HOT AND SWEET SOUP

INGREDIENTS

1.	Capsicum, onion, cabbage and cauliflower (chopped)	50 gm each
2.	Tomato sauce	50 gm
3.	Sugar	2-3 tsp
4.	Corn flour	2-3 tsp
5.	Salt, garam masala	¼ tsp
6.	Vinegar (white) and Soya Sauce	1 tsp
7.	Herbs, oregano, thyme and basil	1 g each

METHOD

(1) Steam all the chopped vegetables for 6-8 min. Strain the fluid and keep the vegetables apart.

(2) Mix tomato sauce, corn flour, sugar and the left over fluid.

(3) Heat it on a low flame. Once it gets boiled add soya sauce, vinegar and sugar. Allow it to heat for 5-7 min. Add the chopped vegetables.

(4) Allow it to simmer on low flame. Add salt and all three herbs.

(5) Serve hot.

Note: Garam Masala: corinander seeds, cumin seeds, black pepper corns, black cumin seeds, dry ginger powder, cardamom, cloves, cinnamon.

MIXED VEGETABLE SOUP

INGREDIENTS

1.	Seasonal vegetables (Cabbage, Cauliflower)	50 gm each
2.	Carrots (medium sized)	2-3
3.	Tomatoes	1-2
4.	Beans	4-5
5.	Salt and black pepper	To taste
6.	Onion (chopped, small size)	1
7.	Vinegar	1 tsp

METHOD

(1) Wash all the vegetables. Cut them into small pieces. Steam cook them in the pressure cooker for 10 min.

(2) Let them cool. Churn them in the mixer and make a thin paste.

(3) Heat vinegar in a pan, add salt, black pepper and the mixed vegetable paste. Bring it to boil for 10-12 min. If thick, add some milk.

(4) Serve streaming hot.

SPAGHETTI SOUP

INGREDIENTS

1.	Spaghetti	50 gm
2.	Green chilly (chopped)	2
3.	Garlic slices (chopped)	10-12
4.	Tomato pulp	200 gm
5.	Herbs basil, thyme, and oregano	1 gm each
6.	Soya sauce	1 tsp
7.	Salt	To taste

METHOD

(1) Boil spaghetti in ½ litre of water. Add ¼ tsp salt while boiling. Let it boil for 10-15 min. Strain and wash it under running tap water.

(2) Take a pan. Heat soya sauce and put tomato pulp. Heat it on low flame. Add garlic and chopped chillies. Keep it on low flame till it becomes thick.

(3) Mix the washed and cooled spaghetti into it. Cover it up and add herbs while on flame.

(4) Remove it from flame, and add salt to taste. Spaghetti hot soup is ready to be served.

MUSHROOM SOUP

INGREDIENTS

1. Fresh mushrooms	200 gm
2. Garlic slices (chopped)	4-5
3. Salt (black), garam masala	¼ tsp
4. Custard powder	1 tsp
5. Sugar	1 tsp

METHOD

(1) Take fresh mushrooms; wash them thoroughly under tap water. Select half of the mushrooms for cooking.

(2) Steam them on low flame for 10-12 min.

(3) Cut rest of the mushrooms into small pieces.

(4) Churn the warm mushrooms in a mixer. Add custard powder and sugar. Churn it again and make a thin paste.

(5) Heat again on low flame for 10-12 min. Add the chopped mushrooms, chopped garlic, salt, sugar and garam masala. Cook them for 10 min on low flame.

(6) Serve piping hot.

Note: Garam Masala: corinander seeds, cumin seeds, black pepper corns, black cumin seeds, dry ginger powder, cardamom, cloves, cinnamon.

CABBAGE SOUP

INGREDIENTS

1.	Cabbage (finely chopped)	200 gm
2.	Carrots (finely chopped, medium)	2
3.	Milk	50 ml
4.	Custard powder	2 tsp
5.	Salt	¼ tsp
6.	Vinegar	1 tsp

METHOD

(1) Steam cook the chopped cabbage and carrots for 10-15 min.

(2) Mix milk, custard powder and make a thin paste.

(3) Mix it with the steamed cabbage and carrots. Put some warm milk to it and bring it to a boil for 10-15 mins.

(4) Add salt and vinegar.

(5) Sever hot.

GROUNDNUT SOUP

INGREDIENTS

1.	Groundnuts (roasted)	100 gm
2.	Milk toned	100 ml
3.	Cardamom	2
4.	Salt and black pepper	To taste
5.	Coconut (grated)	20 gm

METHOD

(1) Soak groundnut in half milk for 12-15 hrs.

(2) Churn it in the mixer. Strain it and keep aside.

(3) Take half of the milk. Bring it to a boil. Add cardamom to the mixture. Keep on low flame till it thickens in consistency.

(4) When ready add salt, black pepper and dress the soup with grated coconut. Also put the remaining milk.

(5) Serve hot.

PUMPKIN AND SWEET PUMPKIN SOUP

INGREDIENTS

1.	Fresh Pumpkin	100 gm
2.	Sweet Pumpkin	200 gm
3.	Salt	To taste
4.	Garlic slices (chopped)	4-5
5.	Sugar	2 tsp
6.	Mustard seeds	10 gm
7.	Cloves	4-5

METHOD

(1) Cut pumpkin and sweet pumpkin into small pieces. Add cloves, mustard seeds and chopped garlic to them. Bring it to a boil in a pressure cooker for 10 min.

(2) Churn it in the mixer and reduce it to a paste.

(3) Bring it to a boil on low flame for 10-12 min. Add salt.

(4) Serve hot.

CURD AND CORIANDER SOUP

INGREDIENTS

1.	Milk	100 ml
2.	Curd	50 gm
3.	Coriander leaves	Few
4.	Mint leaves	Few
5.	Black salt, cumin powder	To taste
6.	Lemon Juice	2 tsp

METHOD

(1) Mix milk and curd and heat them in a pan. Add lemon juice to it. The milk will get separated.

(2) Separate the cheese and left whey.

(3) Make the formed cheese into small cubes.

(4) Grind mint and coriander leaves together. Add salt and cumin powder.

(5) Bring the soup to boil and serve it hot, garnished with cheese cubes and coriander/mint paste.

COCONUT SOUP

INGREDIENTS

1.	Coconut (grated)	200 gm
2.	Milk	50 ml
3.	Sugar	1 tsp
4.	Corn Flour	1 tsp
5.	Salt	To taste
6.	Cloves	4-5

METHOD

(1) Mix milk (half) with grated coconut and churn together in the mixer. Add sugar and corn flour.

(2) Strain this mixture. Keep it on low flame and add cloves, salt.

(3) Let it become thick as you heat.

(4) Serve hot.

MIXED DRY FRUIT SOUP

INGREDIENTS

1.	Almonds	20 g (10-12 pcs)
2.	Cashew nut	20 g (10-15 pcs)
3.	Walnut	50 g
4.	Kishmish	10-12 pcs
5.	Cumin powder	1 tsp
6.	Sugar	2 tsp
7.	Custard powder	1 tsp
8.	Apple (medium sized)	1

METHOD

(1) Soak all the dry fruits together in 500 ml of water overnight.

(2) Bring them to boil for 15-20 mins till all the dry fruits have become soft.

(3) Let them be cool. Grind them in the mixer.

(4) Bring this mixture to boil on low flame. Add custard powder and sugar.

(5) Move it constantly till it becomes thick. Add cumin powder.

(6) Garnish with cut pieces of apple.

(7) Serve hot with a sandwich.

APPLE SOUP

INGREDIENTS

1.	Fresh green apples	500 gm
2.	Salt	1 tsp
3.	Sugar	2 tsp
4.	Custard powder	1 tsp
5.	Corn flour	1 tsp
6.	Almonds (powdered)	10 gm

METHOD

(1) Wash the apples and cut them into small pieces.

(2) Put 1 glass of water in a pressure cooker and the apple pieces and steam them for 10 min.

(3) Allow it to cool. Strain the mixture. Add the remaining mixture in the grinder. Separate out the thick portion and mix it in the strained liquid.

(4) Keep it on low flame. Allow it to boil and while it is boiling add sugar, custard powder and corn flour to make it thick.

(5) Mix the powdered almonds.

(6) Serve steaming hot.

RICE AND BARLEY SOUP

INGREDIENTS

1.	Rice (soaked overnight)	200 gm
2.	Barley (soaked overnight)	50 gm
3.	Milk toned	50 ml
4.	Sugar	2 tsp
5.	Onion (finely chopped, medium)	1
6.	Cabbage (finely chopped)	50 g
7.	Salt black	¼ tsp
8.	Lemon Juice	2 tsp

METHODS:

(1) Soak rice and barley overnight in a clean pan.
(2) Keep it on low flame for 15-20 mins and heat it. Add salt and lemon juice.
(3) The particles of both cereals will get separated. Strain it thoroughly and keep the rice and barley glaciers separately.
(4) Now add milk to this left over water and keep it on low flame.
(5) Once it starts boiling, add cabbage, onion and salt. Allow it to boil. And serve piping hot.
(6) The grains of cereals can be ground to a fine paste and mixed with vegetables as khichdi, or on bread as cereal jam or even cooked as soup and can be taken with curd.

BEANS SOUP

INGREDIENTS

1. Beans red (Rajma), white (lobhiya) and small (Bengal gram) 50 g each
2. Green chilly — 2
3. Garlic slices — 2
4. Ginger — ¼ tsp
5. Lemon Juice — 2 tsp
6. Black salt, cumin powder — To taste
7. Curd — 2-3 tsp

METHOD

(1) Soak all the 3 types of beans overnight. Then add water to them and bring them to a boil.

(2) Strain this mixture. Keep aside the boiled beans.

(3) Put the mixture them on low flame. Add green chillies, ginger, garlic and curd thoroughly beaten. When it becomes thick, add salt, black cumin and lemon juice to it.

(4) Serve hot.

(5) The boiled beans can be used either as salad or can be used as a vegetable dish.

BEETROOT SOUP

INGREDIENTS

1.	Onion (medium size)	2
2.	Maize flour	1 tsp
3.	Beetroot	1
4.	Lemon juice	1 tsp
5.	Vinegar	½ tsp
6.	Salt, black pepper	To taste

METHOD

(1) Grate and boil the beetroot. Keep them aside.

(2) Dry roast the maize flour till it turns golden brown. Keep it aside.

(3) Sauté the onions till light brown. Add a little extra water, beetroot and salt. Cook for 10-15 minutes.

(4) Transfer it to the blender. Churn properly and sieve.

(5) Reboil the mixture.

(6) Remove from flame. Add lemon juice, vinegar and black pepper.

(7) Serve hot.

FRENCH ONION SOUP

INGREDIENTS

1.	Onion (medium sized)	2
2.	Garlic	4-5 cloves
3.	Bay leaf	1
4.	Corn Flour	1 tsp
5.	Pepper corn	1-2
6.	Salt	To taste
7.	Pepper powder	¼ tsp

METHOD

(1) Sauté the chopped onions, crushed garlic cloves, whole spices and seasonings till brown.

(2) Add water, bring it to boil, reduce the heat and simmer for 15-20 minutes. Mix in a blender.

(3) Pass through a sieve. Reboil the mixture and add corn flour paste.

(4) Serve hot in a soup bowl.

GAZPACHO

1.	Tomatoes (chopped)	2
2.	Lemon juice	2 tsp
3.	Vinegar	2 tsp
4.	Onion (finely chopped)	1
5.	Spring onion (chopped)	1
6.	Cucumber (small)	1
7.	Garlic	1 clove
8.	Salt	To taste

METHOD

(1) Liquidize tomatoes, lemon juice, vinegar, onions, and garlic.

(2) To the liquidizer add cucumber and further liquidize.

(3) Add salt and chill it.

(4) Before serving, garnish it with spring onions and the remaining cucumber.

(5) Serve chilled.

GREEN PEAS SOUP

INGREDIENTS

1.	Peas (shredded)	1 cup
2.	Carrot (chopped)	1
3.	Onion (chopped)	1
4.	Mint leaves	A sprig
5.	Corn flour	1 tsp
6.	Salt	To taste
7.	Pepper powder	¼ tsp

METHOD

(1) Sauté chopped onions and carrot.

(2) Add to it peas, mint, pepper, seasonings and water. Cook for 20-30 minutes on slow heat.

(3) Mix it in the blender and strain. Add corn flour dissolved in cold water to make a paste.

(4) Serve hot.

PULSE SOUP

INGREDIENTS

1.	Moong pulse	¼ cup
2.	Urad pulse	20-30 g
3.	Black masar	¼ cup
4.	Ginger paste	¼ tsp
5.	Garlic paste	¼ tsp
6.	Lemon juice	1 tsp
7.	Salt and black pepper	To taste
8.	Pepper corns	4-5
9.	Sugar	2 tsp

METHOD

(1) Soak the pulses overnight. Boil them in the pressure cooker.

(2) Once boiled, strain them so that the solution is separated from the pulse itself.

(3) Allow it to cool, add lemon juice and keep on low flame till it becomes thick.

(4) When the liquid thickens up, add ginger, garlic paste, pepper corn, sugar, and salt. Keep it on low flame for 25-30 minutes.

(5) Serve hot when it becomes thick.

FENUGREEK SOUP

INGREDIENTS

1.	Fenugreek stalks (Methi)	Few
2.	Coriander stalks	Few
3.	Lemon juice	2 tsp
4.	Black salt, cumin powder	To taste
5.	Mustard seeds	Few
6.	Milk	100 ml

METHOD

(1) Heat half of milk in a pan. Add mustard seeds to it.

(2) Boil fenugreek and coriander stalks. Blend it in the mixer.

(3) Strain the mixer.

(4) Put this mixture solution in the milk. Keep it on low flame. Let it boil till it becomes thick.

(5) Add lemon juice, black salt and cumin.

(6) Serve hot.

SOYA SOUP

INGREDIENTS

1.	Soya beans nuggets	50 g
2.	Tomatoes (medium)	2
3.	Sugar	1 tsp
4.	Green chilly	2
5.	Salt	To taste
6.	Cloves	1-2

METHOD

(1) Soak Soya beans overnight. Boil the mixture.

(2) Blend it in the blender.

(3) Strain it through a sieve and keep it aside.

(4) Blanch tomatoes and chillies together. Separate the mixture.

(5) Mix it in the pan containing soya solution.

(6) Bring it to a boil till it becomes thick.

(7) Add sugar and salt to taste before serving.

(8) Serve hot.

TAMARIND SOUP

INGREDIENTS

1.	Tamarind pulp	50 g
2.	Tomato pulp/puree	½ cup
3.	Black salt	To taste
4.	Cumin powder	¼ tsp
5.	Cloves	4-5
6.	Sugar	2 tsp

METHOD

(1) Soak tamarind for few hours. Separate the pulp and fluid.

(2) Boil this liquid till it becomes thick.

(3) Add tomato pulp, cloves, black salt, cumin powder and sugar to it.

(4) Stir it thoroughly and gradually on low flame till it becomes thick.

(5) Serve hot.

part 7
SALADS & DRESSINGS

Salads are misunderstood and are not a component of normal Indian food habits. Salads basically include the vegetables, fruits, soaked moongs, few cereal foods, leaves, herbs, and milk products as dressings.

Some of the commonly cooked salads are:

- Cheese and Peas Salad
- Mushroom & Cabbage Salad
- Fresh Green Salad
- Carrot & Radish Salad
- Chidwa Salad
- Beans Salad
- Corn Salad
- Gramflour Salad
- Hot & Sweet Salad
- Topioca Salad
- Fruit Salad
- Mixed Sprout Salad
- Stuffed Tomato
- Stuffed Capsicum
- Sweet 'n' Sour Salad
- Potato Salad
- Bread Salad
- Cream Salad
- Macaroni Salad
- Chickpea Salad
- Potato Peas Salad
- Minty Fruit Salad
- Sprouted Wheat Salad
- Sweet lime & Cucumber Salad
- Soya Salad
- Wheat & Chick Peas Salad
- Black Chickpea Salad
- Sweet Potato & Beetroot Salad
- Mixed Pulses Salad
- Mixed Green Salad
- Peanut and Cucumber Salad
- Kurkuri Salad

ADVANTAGES OF EATING SALADS

1. It is a good source of roughage which keeps the stomach fit and gives a regulated peristaltic movement to the intestines.
2. It is a low calorie food which is good for cardiac and overweight patients.

3. As a major component of food, it reduces the risk of coronary heart disease, the levels of cholesterol and triglycerides. It is a recommended diet in pregnancy and lactating mothers.
4. It is a recommended food in intestinal disorders when acidity has increased and motility (ability to move independently) of intestines has reduced.
5. It is a complete food for the elderly if taken properly and in a judicious manner.
6. This category of food has been the most neglected aspect of a complete food manual. Let us understand different forms of salads and dressing.

MUSHROOM AND CABBAGE SALAD

INGREDIENTS

1.	Fresh mushrooms	100 gm
2.	Cabbage (finely chopped)	50 gm
3.	Lettuce leaves	5-6
4.	Cabbage leaves	4-5
5.	Salt, cumin (roasted)	To taste
6.	Basil and oregano	1 g each
7.	Curd	40-50 gm
8.	Tomato sauce	20 gm

METHOD

(1) Cut mushrooms into pieces, chop the cabbage finely.
(2) Steam cook both the vegetables for 6-8 minutes.
(3) Keep the curd in a piece of cloth, hang it for 10-15 minutes, use the solid curd for salad.
(4) Mix curd and tomato sauce to make a paste.
(5) Take cabbage and lettuce leaves, wash and set them in a salad plate.
(6) Put steamed cabbage and mushrooms on the leaves and pour curd + tomato sauce mixture on the salad, dress it with salt, cumin, basil, and oregano leaves.
(7) Keep it in the fridge.
(8) Serve either cold or gently warm in the microwave for 30-40 seconds with fresh lime.

CHEESE AND PEAS SALAD

INGREDIENTS

1.	Fresh Peas	100 gm
2.	Milk (Toned)	200 gm
3.	Lemon (small)	1
4.	Tomato Sauce	2 tsp
5.	Cumin (roasted), salt, black pepper	To taste
6.	Cloves	1-2

METHOD

(1) Bring milk to boil, add cloves and lemon to it. The milk will get separated. Strain the ingredients in a cotton cloth and allow it to set. Fresh cheese is ready to be used. Do not throw the fluid left. Keep it in the fridge.

(2) Steam the pealed peas for 4-5 mins.

(3) Set the salad plate and cut the cheese into equal sized cubes. Mix the peas and cheese cubes.

(4) Put Cumin, salt and sauce on them.

(5) Keep it in microwave for 30-40 seconds or serve it just like that.

(6) It should be served with chilled paneer ka pani.

FRESH GREEN SALAD

INGREDIENTS

1.	Fresh seasonal vegetables	250 gm
2.	Onion	1
3.	Tomatoes (medium size)	2
4.	Cucumber (medium size)	1
5.	Garlic slices	4-5
6.	Ginger slices (finely chopped)	5-10 gm
7.	Green chillies	2-3
8.	Beetroot (small)	1
9.	Capsicum (small)	1
10.	Carrots (small)	2
11.	Lemon (medium sized)	1
12.	Black salt, cumin, chat masala	To taste

METHOD

(1) Wash all the vegetables in water, soaked in potassium permanganate thoroughly.

(2) Do not peel off the thick skin of carrot and beetroot. Chop the vegetables finely.

(3) Put ginger, green chillies, and garlic together and make a paste. Put salt, cumin and chat masala.

(4) Mix all the finely chopped vegetables in a bowl. Add lemon juice and dress it with ginger, garlic, chilly paste and serve fresh.

CARROT AND RADISH SALAD

INGREDIENTS

1.	Fresh carrots (medium size)	2
2.	Fresh Radish	1
3.	Pomegranate (peeled)	50 gm
4.	Green chillies (finely chopped)	2-3
5.	Fresh curd	50 gm
6.	Black salt	5-8 gm

METHOD

(1) Grate carrots and radish together. Keep them aside so that extra water flows away.

(2) Take fresh curd and churn it. Mix black salt and chillies to it.

(3) Add grated carrot and radish mixture to it; mix it thoroughly.

(4) Keep it in the fridge, serve chilled, dressed up with peeled pomegranate.

CHIDWA SALAD

INGREDIENTS

1.	Chidwa (beaten rice with pea nuts)	50 gm
2.	Groundnut (roasted)	50 gm
3.	Green chillies (chopped)	2-3
4.	Chickpea (roasted)	20-30 gm
5.	Capsicum (medium size)	1
6.	Carrot (small sized)	2
7.	Fresh green peas	50 g
8.	Ginger (chopped)	10 gm
9.	Garlic (paste)	4-5 slices
10.	Lemon (medium sized)	1
11.	Salt, black pepper, cumin	To taste
12.	Onion (small, chopped)	1
13.	Tomato (small, chopped)	1

METHOD

(1) Sieve chidwa (beaten rice with pea nuts) and roasted chickpea together to remove the fine dust.
(2) Take a non stick pan, allow it to heat and put chidwa and roasted chickpea in it. Roast it for 5-10 minutes till it crackles.
(3) Take a bowl, add chopped capsicum, onion, tomatoes, carrots, ginger and mix it with roasted chickpea chidwa mixture. Add lemon, salt and black pepper.
(4) Server either this way or heat in the microwave for 30 seconds. Serve with fresh lime juice.

EXCELLENT IN:

1. Diabetes
2. Hypertension
3. Cardiac patients
4. Obesity

BEANS SALAD

INGREDIENTS

1.	Red beans (rajma)	50 gm
2.	White beans (lobhiya)	50 gm
3.	Bengal gram pulse	50 gm
4.	Onion (Finely chopped, medium)	1
5.	Tomatoes (Finely chopped, medium)	2
6.	Ginger slices (chopped)	4-5
7.	Green chillies (chopped)	1-2
8.	Lemon (small)	1
9.	Black salt, black pepper	To taste
10.	White vinegar	1 tsp

METHOD

(1) Soak all the beans together in water for 3-4 hours. Then add vinegar, chopped ginger and green chillies and steam cook it. Bring it to boil.
(2) Strain the beans and keep aside the fluid leftover (beans soup).
(3) Mix beans with onion, tomatoes, add black salt, black pepper and lemon according to taste.
(4) Serve with the beans soup.

EXCELLENT IN:

1. Growing children
2. Pregnancy
3. Cardiac patients
4. Diabetes

CORN SALAD

INGREDIENTS

1.	Corn (boiled)	100 gm
2.	Potatoes (finely chopped, boiled)	1
3.	Tomatoes (finely chopped)	1
4.	Green chillies (finely chopped)	2
5.	Bread crumbs	50 g
6.	Milk toned	½ cup
7.	Corn flour	1 tsp
8.	Lemon juice	2 tsp
9.	Coriander leaves (chopped)	A few
10.	Salt, black pepper	To taste

METHOD

(1) Mix milk and corn flour to make a thin solution.

(2) Add chopped chillies, potatoes and tomatoes and bake them for 10 minutes.

(3) Roast bread crumbs dry on the tawa and add to the baking bowl.

(4) Soak corn in lemon juice for 10 minutes and add it into the bowl. To taste, add salt, black pepper and lemon. Garnish it with coriander leaves and serve hot.

GRAMFLOUR SALAD

INGREDIENTS

1.	Gramflour	100 gm
2.	Beans (finely chopped)	30 gm
3.	Peas	50 gm
4.	Potatoes	1
5.	Tomatoes	1
6.	Lemon juice	2 tsp
7.	Corn flour	1 tsp
8.	Tomato sauce	50 gm
9.	Baking powder	pinch
10.	Salt, black pepper	To taste
11.	Herbs: basil, oregano, thyme	Pinch of all 3

METHOD

(1) Steam all chopped vegetables except tomatoes.

(2) Make a thin batter of gramflour, add lemon juice, baking powder, salt, all 3 herbs, black pepper, and salt to it.

(3) Mix tomato sauce and corn flour and heat them in a pan till it becomes thick.

(4) Drain the steamed vegetables and keep the left over soup.

(5) Put all the vegetables in the batter and bake them for 8 minutes.

(6) Serve steaming hot, garnished with cold tomato sauce and vegetable soup.

HOT AND SWEET SALAD

INGREDIENTS

1.	Macaroni or spaghetti (boiled)	100 gm
2.	Tomatoes (finely chopped, medium)	4
3.	Garlic (finely chopped)	4-5
4.	green chillies (finely chopped)	2
5.	Basil, oregano, thyme	Pinch of all 3
6.	Capsicum (chopped, small)	2
7.	Salt and black pepper, sugar	1 tsp
8.	Vinegar, Soya sauce	1 tsp each

METHOD

(1) Boil the macaroni or spaghetti in ½ litre of water. Put ¼ tsp of salt, cook it for 5-10 min.

(2) Drain the macaroni and wash it under cool water.

(3) Take a non-stick pan, add vinegar and finely chopped tomatoes, garlic and chillies to it. Cook it under cover; reduce the tomatoes to a paste and add all 3 herbs. Cook it for 15-20 minutes.

(4) Add boiled macaroni, vinegar, salt, black pepper, and sugar.

(5) Garnish it with capsicum and serve hot.

TOPIOCA SALAD

INGREDIENTS

1. Sabudana — 50 g
2. Beans, capsicum, tomatoes and onions (finely shopped)
3. Boiled peas — 50 g
4. Cheese (cottage) — 50 g
5. Coriander leaves — Few
6. Salt and black pepper — To taste
7. Lemon juice — 1 tsp

METHOD

(1) Soak Topioca in water for 30 minutes. Drain the dana and keep aside the left over liquid.

(2) Steam all the vegetables together and mix them with soaked topioca.

(3) Heat a pan, add lemon juice, salt and black pepper, and topioca mixture. Heat it for 7-8 minutes.

(4) Garnish with cheese and coriander leaves.

(5) Serve hot with topioca soup.

FRUIT SALAD

INGREDIENTS

1.	Seasonal fruits: Papaya	100 gm
2.	Pineapple	200 gm
3.	Oranges (medium)	2
4.	Apple	2
5.	Grapes	Few
6.	Pineapple	2-3 slices
7.	Banana	2 pieces
8.	Milk	50 ml
9.	Sugar powder	To Taste

METHOD

(1) Peel papaya, banana, orange, and apple. Cut them into slices of equal size. Add grapes.

(2) Peel pineapple, slice it and dip it in milk for 10 min. Keep it in fridge.

(3) Mix well the fruits in a bowl. Add sugar and pour milk. Serve it chilled with garnished pineapple slices.

MIXED SPROUT SALAD

INGREDIENTS

1.	Green moong pulse	100 gm
2.	Black moong pulse	50 g
3.	Lemon juice	2 tsp
4.	Onions (chopped, small)	2
5.	Tomatoes (chopped, small)	2
6.	Green chillies (chopped)	2
7.	Salt, roasted cumin seeds	To taste

METHOD

(1) Soak both the pulses separately in water for 2-3 hours. Strain and keep in a wet cloth in sunlight. Allow the sprouts to come out.

(2) Mix both the pulses together and wash thoroughly under running water.

(3) Steam gently for 5-6 min.

(4) Take a bowl and and add to it the chopped onions, tomatoes, chillies, and pulses. Serve it either cold or warm with lemon, salt and cumin.

STUFFED TOMATO SALAD

INGREDIENTS

1.	Fresh tomatoes (medium sized)	6
2.	Fresh green peas	100 gm
3.	Curd	50 gm
4.	Cucumber slices	8-10
5.	Tomato sauce	50 g
6.	Onion sliced	50 g
7.	Capsicum slices (medium sized)	1
8.	Salt, cumin powder	To taste

METHOD

(1) Wash tomatoes, cut the top and scoop the pulp of tomatoes. Keep the pulp aside.

(2) Make a thick batter of curd, mix the tomato pulp and fresh peas.

(3) Fill this paste into the tomatoes. Keep it in the microwave, heat for 30-50 seconds.

(4) Arrange the tomatoes in the bowl. Garnish with slices of capsicum, onion, and cucumber. Sprinkle salt and cumin powder. Serve hot either with tomato or Coriander Dip.

STUFFED CAPSICUM SALAD

INGREDIENTS

1.	Capsicum (medium sized)	4-5
2.	Potatoes (boiled, small sized)	2
3.	Cheese cottage	50 g
4.	Lemon juice	2 tsp
5.	Salt, black pepper	To taste

METHOD

(1) Wash the capsicum and scoop it out removing the top of capsicum.

(2) Mix cheese and potatoes, and lemon juice, salt and black pepper.

(3) Make round balls and fill the capsicum with the mixture.

(4) Heat in the oven for 6-8 minutes.

(5) Serve hot with tomato sauce.

SWEET 'N' SOUR SALAD

INGREDIENTS

1.	Sweet pumpkin	200 gm
2.	Onion slices (medium)	1
3.	Green chillies (chopped)	2
4.	Mustard seeds	10-15 gm
5.	Sugar	2 tsp
6.	Lemon juice	2 tsp
7.	Drum sticks	2
8.	Salt, cumin powder	To taste

METHOD

(1) Wash the pumpkin and cut it into small cubical slices. Steam it for 5-10 min.

(2) Take a pan, add sugar and water. Heat it for 2-3 min. Add mustard seeds till it pops.

(3) Cut drumsticks into small pieces. Put them in the pan. Cook them for 10-15 min. Add lemon juice when they become soft.

(4) Mix drumsticks and sweet pumpkin. Add salt, cumin, and lemon juice. Garnish with chillies and chopped onion slices.

STUFFED POTATO SALAD

INGREDIENTS

1.	Potatoes (small size)	5-8
2.	Macaroni (boiled)	50 g
3.	Pulse chickpea (soaked)	50 g
4.	Onion slices (medium)	1
5.	Vinegar, Soya sauce	1 tsp each
6.	Cabbage leaves	4-5
7.	Salt, black pepper, cumin	To taste

METHOD

(1) Peel the potatoes. Steam cook them for 8-10 min. Cut the potatoes into 2 pieces.
(2) Bring macaroni to boil. After boiling it, add vinegar and soya sauce.
(3) Steam chickpea pulse for 10-15 minutes.
(4) Mix macaroni and pulse chickpea. Add salt, black pepper, and cumin to the mixture.
(5) Stuff the potatoes with this mixture and join both the cut pieces with a tooth pick.
(6) Keep it in microwave. Heat it for 1-2 minutes.
(7) Take cabbage leaves, dress them in the salad bowl. Garnish with onion slices and serve hot.

BREAD SALAD

INGREDIENTS

1.	Bread crumbs fresh	100 g
2.	Macaroni (boiled)	50 g
3.	Onion, tomatoes (chopped)	1
4.	Green chillies (chopped, medium)	1-2
5.	Lemon juice	2 tsp
6.	Cottage cheese	50 g
7.	Salt, black pepper	To taste
8.	Basil, oregano, thyme	Pinch of all 3

METHOD

(1) Boil macaroni and add the 3 herbs while boiling it.

(2) Strain the mixture. Add chopped onions, tomatoes, chillies, and bread crumbs to it.

(3) Put lemon juice, salt and pepper.

(4) Garnish the salad with grated cottage cheese.

CREAM SALAD

INGREDIENTS

1.	Cabbage (chopped)	50 gm
2.	Peas fresh	50 gm
3.	Capsicum	50 gm
4.	Cauliflower	50 gm
5.	Tomato sauce	100 gm
6.	Cream of low fat	100 gm
7.	Cumin powder, black pepper, salt, garam masala	To taste

METHOD

(1) Mix all vegetables and steam cook it for 5-10 minutes.

(2) Strain the vegetables. Do not throw the left over. Mix salt in it to serve it as a soup.

(3) Mix sauce, cream, cumin powder, black pepper, salt, and garam masala. Make a batter and churn it.

(4) Mix the vegetables thoroughly with the cream batter. Keep it in the fridge and serve cool.

Note: Garam Masala: corinander seeds, cumin seeds, black pepper corns, black cumin seeds, dry ginger powder, cardamom, cloves, cinnamon.

MACARONI SALAD

INGREDIENTS

1.	Macaroni	50 g
2.	Onion (finely chopped, medium sized)	1
3.	Tomato (finely chopped, medium sized)	1
4.	Peas (boiled)	50 g
5.	Cabbage (shredded finely)	50 g
6.	Carrot (finely chopped)	50 g
7.	Soya sauce	1 tsp
8.	Vinegar	2 tsp
9.	Tomato sauce	To taste
10.	Curd (thick)	50 g
11.	Salt, black pepper	To taste
12.	Lemon juice	1 tsp

METHOD

(1) Boil macaroni in a water on low flame. Add lemon juice while boiling so that the macaroni does not stick to each other. Wash it under running water.

(2) Put curd and vinegar in a sauce pan. Allow it to heat on low flame. Put all the vegetables in it and cook it on low flame with the lid covered.

(3) Keep it on low flame for 15-20 minutes and add vinegar, tomato sauce, and soya sauce. Mix it thoroughly with cooked the macaroni.

(4) Serve it hot in the salad bowl with salt and black pepper.

CHICKPEA SALAD

INGREDIENTS

1.	White chickpea (soaked overnight)	100 gm
2.	Ginger (finely grated)	50 g
3.	Coriander leaves	Few
4.	Lemon juice	2 tsp
5.	Tamarind water	2-3 tsp
6.	Potatoes (boiled, finely chopped, medium)	1
7.	Green chilly (chopped, small)	1
8.	Black salt, Cumin powder	To taste

METHOD

(1) Soak chickpea overnight and boil it till it becomes soft.

(2) Mash it to a soft paste.

(3) Add to it lemon juice, tamarind water, and mix it with chopped potatoes, green chillies, salt, and cumin.

(4) Heat it in a pan.

(5) Serve it hot garnished with coriander leaves and ginger. It can be served as such or with hot buns.

POTATO PEAS SALAD

INGREDIENTS

1. Potatoes (boiled)	2-3 pcs
2. Peas (boiled)	½ cup
3. Salt	To taste
4. Chat masala	¼ tsp
5. Ginger slices (long)	2-3
6. Lemon (small)	1

METHOD

(1) Mix all the ingredients together and heat on low flame.

(2) Serve hot.

MINTY FRUIT SALAD

INGREDIENTS

1. Black grapes — ½ cup
2. Green grapes — ½ cup
3. Cherries — ½ cup
4. Lime juice — 1 tsp
5. Mint leaves (chopped) — 1 tsp
6. Musk melon (small) — 1

METHOD

(1) Cut the melon and remove the seeds. Peel the melon and cut into small pieces.

(2) Put these pieces in a serving bowl. Spread both types of grapes and cherries over it.

(3) Scatter the grated mint on the fruits.

(4) Squeeze lemon on fruits as well.

(5) Lastly garnish it with mint leaves and serve chilled.

SPROUTED WHEAT SALAD

INGREDIENTS

1. Cabbage (shredded)	1 cup
2. Mint leaves (chopped)	1 tsp
3. Sprouted wheat	½ cup
4. Cucumber (peeled and diced)	1 ½ cup
5. Pepper	¼ tsp
6. Lemon juice	3 lemons
7. Tomato (diced)	½ cup
8. Salt	To taste

METHOD

(1) Put the sprouted wheat in boiled water for 25 minutes and cover it.

(2) After soaking, drain the water. Add cucumber with salt to it.

(3) In a bowl add lemon juice, garlic, salt, and pepper and mix it well.

(4) Transfer it to a sprout bowl and blend well.

(5) Add tomatoes, cucumber, cabbage, mix and arrange the seasonings accordingly.

SWEET LIME AND CUCUMBER SALAD

INGREDIENTS

1. Cucumber (grated) — ½ cup
2. Sweet lime juice — 1 cup
3. Salt and black pepper — To taste
4. Gelatin — 1 tsp

METHOD

(1) Add gelatin to ¼ cup sweet lime juice and warm it a little.

(2) When cool add remaining juice and refrigerate it.

(3) Take it out after 15-20 minutes or when set. Then, add to it grated cucumber.

(4) Put the mixture in the empty peel of sweet lime.

(5) Again refrigerate it and serve chilled.

SEASONED PAPAYA SALAD

INGREDIENTS

1.	Papaya (sliced)	2 cups
2.	Garlic	2-3 cloves
3.	Whole red chillies (soaked in water)	2
4.	Lime juice (medium size)	3 lemon
5.	Sugar	1 tsp
6.	Tamarind juice	1 tsp
7.	Pepper corns	3-4
8.	Salt	To taste
9.	Cucumber (sliced)	½ cup
10.	Tomato (sliced, medium sized)	1

METHOD

(1) Make a paste of red chillies, garlic, and pepper corns.

(2) Add papaya, tomato, cucumber, sugar and salt and pound it gently.

(3) Now add lemon juice, sliced lemon, tamarind juice and pound it further.

(4) Serve it.

SOYA SALAD

INGREDIENTS

1.	Soya chunks (fine)	100 gm
2.	Fresh peas (boiled)	½ cup
3.	Boiled potato (sliced)	½ cup
4.	Green chillies (finely chopped)	2
5.	Coriander leaves (finely chopped)	Few
6.	Lemon juice	2 tsp
7.	Mint leaves	Few
8.	Black salt and cumin	To taste

METHOD

(1) Soak soya bean for 2-3 hours and then bring it to boil on low heat. Once it is boiled. Cool it and strain it through a sieve.

(2) In a bowl add soya beans, chopped potatoes, chillies, peas, salt and cumin.

(3) Put it in a bowl, heat it in the microwave oven for 30-40 seconds.

(4) Serve warm, garnished with mint leaves.

WHEAT AND CHICK PEAS SALAD

INGREDIENTS

1.	Coriander leaves	Few
2.	Spring onion	1
3.	Chick pea sprouts	100 gm
4.	Wheat sprouts	100 gm
5.	Pineapple slices, tomato, cucumber	Few
6.	Lemon juice	2 tsp
7.	Chilly powder	½ tsp
8.	Black pepper powder, salt	To taste

METHOD

(1) Dice the cucumber, tomato, and pineapple.

(2) Mix the sprouts with the vegetables along with chopped spring onion and coriander leaves in a bowl.

(3) Mix together lemon juice, chilly powder, salt, and black pepper.

(4) Add this to the vegetables in the bowl and toss well before serving.

BLACK CHICKPEA AND TOMATO SALAD

Ingredients

1.	Black Chickpea (soaked overnight)	100 gm
2.	Tomatoes (medium)	2
3.	Green chilly (chopped)	1
4.	Coriander leaves	few
5.	Amla (steamed)	1-2
6.	Lemon juice	1 tsp
7.	Salt and black cumin powder	To taste
8.	Walnuts (soaked)	few

METHOD

(1) Soak chickpea overnight. Then boil them. Later, strain them and separate the soup.

(2) Add to the boiled chickpea, green chilly, coriander leaves and amla in a bowl. Slice half of the tomatoes.

(3) Cut the other half of the tomatoes into small round pieces. Add lemon juice, coriander leaves, salt, black cumin and walnuts.

(4) Add to the chickpea mixture and mix them thoroughly. Slightly warm it before serving.

SWEET POTATO AND BEETROOT SALAD

INGREDIENTS

1.	Sweet potato (boiled medium sized)	2
2.	Beetroot (sliced, medium sized)	1
3.	Mint leaves (chopped)	A few
4.	Lemon juice	2 tsp
5.	Black salt	To taste
6.	Cumin powder	¼ tsp

METHOD

(1) Soak beetroot slices in water for ½ hour separately. Put few drops of lime juice over the beet root.

(2) Peel the sweet potato and cut it into small pieces.

(3) Take a salad bowl, mix slices of beet root and sweet potato. Mix mint leaves, cumin powder, black salt and lemon juice into it.

(4) Serve it hot with either soup or bread.

MIXED PULSES SALAD

INGREDIENTS

1.	Pulse Arhar	50 g
2.	Pulse Urad	50 g
3.	Pulse Moong (broken)	50 g
4.	Onion (chopped finely, medium sized)	1
5.	Ginger (chopped finely)	1 tsp
6.	Lemon juice	2 tsp
7.	Tamarind juice	2 tsp
8.	Cabbage (shredded)	½ cup
9.	Black pepper and salt	To taste

METHOD

(1) Soak all the pulses separately overnight.

(2) Steam them separately.

(3) Sieve and use the left over as soup.

(4) Mix ginger, onion, cabbage and salt to the pulses in a bowl. Add black pepper, lemon juice, and tamarind juice to the mixture.

(5) Serve hot.

GREEN SALAD

INGREDIENTS

1.	Spinach leaves	10-12
2.	Methi leaves	Few
3.	Sarson leaves	Few
4.	Peas (boiled)	½ cup
5.	Mint leaves	Few
6.	Chenopodium leaves	Few
7.	Lemon juice	1 tsp
8.	Soya sauce	½ tsp
9.	Vinegar	1 tsp
10.	Salt	To taste

METHOD

(1) Clean all the leaves and wash them thoroughly.
(2) Steam the spinach leaves gently so that it does not loose its colour.
(3) Steam all the vegetables and ground them to a paste.
(4) Mix them with peas and add soya sauce and vinegar. Make small round balls of the mixture.
(5) Spread spinach leaves in a bowl and arrange the balls on them. Sprinkle lemon juice and salt.
(6) Serve hot.

PEANUT AND CUCUMBER SALAD

INGREDIENTS

1.	Cucumber (medium sized)	2
2.	Mustard seeds	Few
3.	Peanuts (roasted)	½ cup
4.	Mint leaves (chopped)	A few
5.	Lemon juice	2 tsp
6.	Curd	2 tsp
7.	Salt and cumin powder	To taste

METHOD

(1) Cut cucumber into small pieces along with the peel.

(2) Heat it in pan of water on low flame till it gets soft.

(3) Put curd in a pan along with and mustard seeds. When it starts sprinkling, add cucumber slices and peanuts to it.

(4) Mix them thoroughly. Add lemon juice, mint leaves, salt and cumin.

(5) Warm it slightly to serve fresh.

CRUNCHY SALAD

INGREDIENTS

1. Sabudana (roasted) — 50 g
2. Chickpea (roasted) — ½ cup
3. Peanuts (roasted) — ½ cup
4. Jal jeera — ¼ tsp
5. Lemon juice — 1 tsp
6. Wheat (roasted) — ½ tsp
7. Onion (chopped) — 1
8. Tomato (chopped) — 1
9. Green chilly — 1

METHOD

(1) Mix all the ingredients together and warm slightly in the microwave for 30-40 seconds.

(2) Serve warm before meals.

ESSENTIALS OF A GOOD SALAD:

1. It should give a variety.
2. The fruits and vegetables selected should be of good quality.
3. Make it more colourful by adding different vegetables and fruits.
4. Do not use too much of condiments and spices.
5. Do not use many garnishes.
6. A good salad is one which is not only an appetizer but is nourishing also.

part 8
SNACKS

Snacks are a very important part of Indian cuisine. Snacks are the most desirable part of menu which have to be added carefully in the diet schedule of patients. Keeping in mind the minimum oil cooking, such snacks have been selected as to give a variety to the menu. Special emphasis has been given to the individual base selection for different snacks.

The recipes of snacks which are given in this book has been listed below.

- Shan-E-Bread
- Bread Poha
- Bread Pizza
- Bread Rolls
- Club Sandwiches
- Cheese Cabbage Sandwiches
- Tomato Onion Sandwiches
- Merry Go Sandwiches
- Grilled Sandwiches
- Toast a Taste
- Pinhole Sandwich
- Bread Pakora
- Gramflour Pancake
- Gramflour Rolls
- Gramflour Bread
- Navratan Gramflour
- Gramflour Nuts
- Gramflour Pakoras
- Veg. Upma
- Veg Seekh Kabab
- Veg Shammi Kabab
- Veg Pancake
- Veg Noodles
- Upma
- Stuffed Egg White
- Steamed Cabbage Rolls
- Cutlets
- Spicy Spinach Balls
- Idli
- Roasted Chickpea Brittle
- Rice Moong Pulse Idli
- Pancake
- Vermicelli
- Pepper Vermicelli
- Pao Bhaji

- Moong Pulse Dhokla
- Dahi Vada
- Burger
- Lemon Vermicelli
- Dosa
- Baked Samosa
- Baked Buns
- Bhel Puri
- Chidwa (beaten rice with pea nuts)
- Canopy
- Kachori
- Tofu Pakoras
- Mixed Veg Pakoras
- Baby Corn Pakoras
- Chatpate Corns
- Arvi Patta Pakoras
- Crispy Pineapple

PREPARATION FROM BREAD

A wonderful complete food that contains a complete composite of proteins, vitamins and roughage. A simple carbohydrate turned into SHAH-E-SNACK is a wonderful evening snack and can be used as a full meal also.

SHAN-E-BREAD

INGREDIENTS

1.	Bread slices (white)	6-8
2.	Capsicum, carrots, spring onion (chopped)	50 gm each
3.	Green chillies (chopped)	1
4.	Flour	100 gm
5.	Salt	To taste
6.	Dry methi leaves	½ tsp
7.	Red chilly flakes	Pinch
8.	Curd	2-3 tsp
9.	Oregano	Pinch

METHOD

1. Mix curd and flour and add water to make a semi paste. Add all finely chopped veggies with salt and methi leaves.
2. Keep the non-stick pan on low flame. Add one drop of oil, clean it and pour a few spoons of milk to form a base for cooking.
3. Keep the bread slices in the non-stick pan and add the flour batter on the slices and spread it like a paste on the slices.
4. Allow it to heat on low flame, once it turns brown on one side, add chilly flakes and oregano.
5. Let it remain on the flame for 4-5 min.
6. Serve it hot with pudina Dip or sauce as per taste.

BREAD POHA

INGREDIENTS

1.	Bread cut into small square pieces	3-4 slices
2.	Onion (finely chopped, medium sized)	1
3.	Tomato (medium sized)	1
4.	Peas green (shelled)	½ cup
5.	Green chillies (chopped)	2
6.	Curd (churned)	½ cup
7.	Ginger slices (chopped)	6-8
8.	Salt	To Taste
9.	Garam masala	To Taste
10.	Tomato sauce	¼ cup
11.	Soya sauce	1 tsp

METHOD

(1) Put curd in a sauce pan and allow it to heat on low flame.
(2) Add chopped onions, simmer them on low heat till they changes their colour.
(3) Add peas and cook them on low flame.
(4) When peas get cooked add tomatoes and salt.
(5) Cook it on slow flame till it leaves water and becomes thick.
(6) When the mixture becomes thick add soya sauce, garam masala and the bread slices.
(7) Mix it thoroughly and allow it to heat on low flame till it gets cooked.
(8) Garnish with ginger slices and serve hot with tomato sauce.

Note: Garam Masala: corinander seeds, cumin seeds, black pepper corns, black cumin seeds, dry ginger powder, cardamom, cloves, cinnamon.

BREAD PIZZA

INGREDIENTS

1.	Brown bread	3-4 slices
2.	Capsicum (finely chopped, small sized)	1
3.	Onion (finely chopped, small sized)	1
4.	Carrots (finely chopped, small sized)	2
5.	Tomatoes (Finely chopped)	2
6.	Cheese slices (of low fat, small sized)	1
7.	Salt	To taste
8.	Garam masala	To taste
9.	Lemon juice	2 tsp
10.	Milk	¼ cup
11.	Tomato sauce	3-4 tsp

METHOD

(1) Heat milk in a pan on low flame. Add onions and saute till any changes any colour. When slightly cooked add all the vegetables one by one and allow them to be cooked on low flame for 10-12 minutes.
(2) When cooked thoroughly add garam masala and lemon juice.
(3) Arrange bread slices in a microwave dish and put sauce on the cooked vegetables.
(4) Grate cheese and garnish the vegetable slices.
(5) Heat in a microwave for 1-2 minutes.
(6) Bread pizza is ready to be served. If microwave is not available, then heat bread slices on low flame under a cover, allow them to become crisp and serve hot.

Note: Garam Masala: corinander seeds, cumin seeds, black pepper corns, black cumin seeds, dry ginger powder, cardamom, cloves, cinnamon.

BREAD ROLLS

INGREDIENTS

1.	Boiled potatoes (medium sized)	2-3
2.	Shelled peas (boiled)	½ cup
3.	Onion (chopped finely, small sized)	2
4.	Green chillies (chopped, small sized)	2
5.	Coriander leaves	A few
6.	Mint leaves	A few
7.	Cottage Cheese	50 g
8.	Bread slices	5-6
9.	Milk	5-6 tsp
10.	Salt	To taste
11.	Cumin powder	¼ tsp
12.	Tomato sauce	To serve

METHOD

(1) Heat water in a pan and add chopped onions and peas.
(2) When they become soft add green chillies and cumin powder.
(3) Cut potatoes into small pieces and add to this mixture.
(4) Keep it on low flame till the flavour is gained.
(5) Now add cheese and salt. Garnish with coriander leaves and mint leaves. Mix it thoroughly again.
(6) Soak bread slices in water and put this mixture on the soaked bread.
(7) Role the bread slices in your palm so that the water is drained out and give them the shapes of a round or oblong roll.
(8) Put milk in a microwave dish and heat it for 2 min. Keep these rolls in the dish base and heat them for 6-8 minutes on both sides.
(9) Serve hot with tomato sauce.

CLUB SANDWICHES

SANDWICHES

It is the most widely applicable of oil free cuisine which can be prepared with one common base but different fillings. Let us have a look on different variety of sandwiches available with us.

INGREDIENTS

1.	Bread slice (medium size)	6
2.	Cheese slice	1
3.	Cucumber slices	5-6
4.	Tomato slices	5-6
5.	Tomato sauce	2-3 tsp
6.	Pudina Dip	4-5 tsp
7.	Cabbage (grated)	50 g

METHOD

(1) Arrange bread slices in a row and apply sauce on one, pudina Dip on other and the cheese slice on the third one.

(2) Garnish each slice with cucumber, tomato and cabbage

(3) Club each slice one over the other and serve it either with cold coffee or soup.

CHEESE CABBAGE SANDWICH

INGREDIENTS

1. Cabbage (grated) — ½ cup
2. Beetroot (grated) — ½ cup
3. Capsicum (finely chopped, small) — 1
4. Curd thick — 1 cup
5. Bread slices — 4
6. Black salt and cumin — To taste
7. Tomato sauce — 5-6 tsp

METHOD

(1) Grate cabbage, beetroot and chop capsicum finely.

(2) Steam them well and add black salt and cumin.

(3) Hang curd in a cloth till the entire water is drained out.

(4) Mix all the steamed vegetables with curd and tomato sauce.

(5) Arrange the slices one over the other with the filling of the mixture.

(6) Wrap it in a foil and serve fresh with lime water.

TOMATO ONION SANDWICH

INGREDIENTS

1.	Bread	4
2.	Onion (round slices)	4-5
3.	Coriander leaves (chopped)	Few
4.	Tomato (slices round)	4-5
5.	Salt, cumin powder	To taste
6.	Tomato sauce	To serve

METHOD

(1) Arrange onion and tomato slices between bread slices. Put salt and cumin on them.

(2) Garnish with coriander leaves.

(3) Heat the tawa and put the bread slices directly on it.

(4) Heat it from both sides till it becomes crisp.

(5) Serve hot with tomato sauce.

MERRY GO SANDWICHES

INGREDIENTS

1. Bread slices — 6-8
2. Cabbage (shredded) — ½ cup
3. Carrot (grated) — 1
4. Salt, cumin, and garam masala — To taste
5. Cheese (grated) — 50 g
6. Peas (shredded, boiled) — ½ cup
7. Vinegar — 2-3 tsp
8. Curd(hung) — ½ cup
9. Tomato sauce — 5-6 tsp
10. Fresh cheese (grated) — 50 g

METHOD

(1) Cut the bread slices round with the help of a bowl.
(2) Mix all the chopped vegetables and heat them in a pan on low flame so that they become slightly tender.
(3) Mix hang curd to them and add salt, cumin and garam masala, vinegar and tomato sauce.
(4) Arrange this mixture in a bowl and garnish with fresh cheese. Leave some cheese spare for the slices.
(5) Put grated cheese into round cut slices. Arrange it in the dish.
(6) Put it in the microwave and heat for 40-60 seconds.
(7) Serve hot with tomato sauce.

Note: Garam Masala: corinander seeds, cumin seeds, black pepper corns, black cumin seeds, dry ginger powder, cardamom, cloves, cinnamon.

GRILLED SANDWICHES

INGREDIENTS

1.	Bread slices	6
2.	Peas (shelled, boiled)	50 g
3.	Potatoes (boiled)	1 cut into fine pieces
4.	Cumin	¼ tsp
5.	Cheese (grated)	50 gm
6.	Green chillies (chopped)	2
7.	Tomato sauce	To taste
8.	Coriander leaves (chopped)	Few
9.	Black salt, garam masala	To taste

Note: Garam Masala: corinander seeds, cumin seeds, black pepper corns, black cumin seeds, dry ginger powder, cardamom, cloves, cinnamon.

METHOD

(1) Heat water in a pan and add cumin and sauté it.
(2) Add boiled cut potatoes, onions, and peas with green chillies and tomato sauce.
(3) Heat them on low flame for 10 minutes. Once it is cool, add cheese, garam masala and black salt.
(4) Fill this mixture in between the bread slices and keep it in the grill or the sandwich toaster.
(5) Serve it hot with tomato sauce.

NOTE: In place of potatoes and peas, cheese, cabbage or carrot can also be used as a filling.

TOAST A TASTE

INGREDIENTS

1.	Bread slices	4
2.	Potatoes (medium size, boiled)	2
3.	Cheese (grated) (instead of butter)	50 g
4.	Rings of onion, capsicum, mushroom	A few
5.	Cheese cubes	2
6.	Salt	To taste
7.	White pepper	Pinch
8.	Mustard powder	Pinch
9.	Tomato ketchup	4 tsp

METHOD

(1) Take bread and spread cheese on it. Add mashed potatoes on it and spread them.

(2) On this mixture spread 1 tsp tomato ketchup.

(3) Add onion rings and capsicum rings.

(4) Then again spread cheese on it.

(5) Now add a pinch of salt, white pepper, and mustard powder.

(6) Preheat the oven at 220°C for 10 minutes. Grease the grill and heat both the elements.

(7) After heating, put a drop of ketchup at the center and coriander leaves can also be used for garnishing.

(8) Serve hot with tomato sauce.

PIN HOLE SANDWICHES

INGREDIENTS

1. Bread loaf — 1
2. Butter — As required

MULTICOLOURED:

Green: 2 tsp mint Dip, grated cucumber, capsicum or cabbage

Red: 2 tsp ketchup, red colour, grated beet root, bits of tomato

Yellow: Yellow colour, 1 small paneer or cheese cube, pinch of black pepper, salt to taste, butter 1 tsp

Filling: Spread butter on each slice evenly.

Green Filing: Cucumber with green skin, grated. To this add 1 tsp salt. Mix it thoroughly. Remove water from cucumber by tilting it and not by squeezing it.

Red Filling: In ketchup add 2 drops of red colour. Cut bits of tomato and add a pinch of sauce in it.

Yellow Filling: 1/3rd cup of paneer for 1 sandwich. To this add butter, salt, pepper, 4-5 drops of yellow colour. Mix it well.

METHOD

(1) Spread green Dip on 1/3rd portion of bread. On it add cucumber or cabbage or capsicum.
(2) On the 2nd portion, add yellow mixture and press on the 3rd portion. Add ketchup and on it tomato pieces or red chopped carrot.
(3) Roll it and press the end slightly and now keep it in the freezing chamber for ½ hour or maximum for an hour wrapped in foil.
(4) After that when it is set, cut it and keep it in the first shelf with the help of a wet knife. Cut smoothly into round wheels.
(5) Arrange it on a cabbage bed and serve with tomato ketchup.

BREAD PAKORA

INGREDIENTS

1.	Bread slices	2-3
2.	Gramflour	½ cup
3.	Salt	To taste
4.	Cumin powder	¼ tsp
5.	Water	½ cup
6.	Soda bicarbonate	Pinch
7.	Potato (small, boiled, mashed)	1
8.	Capsicum (chopped, small)	1
9.	Cheese cube(grated/sliced)	2
10.	Green chillies (chopped)	1
11.	Pudina Dip	To serve
12.	Ketchup	To serve

METHOD

(1) Cut the slices into four squares.
(2) Mix Gramflour, salt, cumin powder, soda bicarbonate, chopped chillies and water to make a thick batter.
(3) Mix potatoes and chopped capsicum together and apply it on each bread slice and close them together.
(4) Dip each slice in the Gramflour batter and keep it in the microwave dish (oven).
(5) Heat it at 950 watts for 4-5 minutes on both sides and serve hot with pudina Dip and tomato ketchup.

GRAMFLOUR PANCAKE

Gramflour is one of the cereal ingredients which is used as a base for many snacks. It is prepared by roasting and grinding Chickpea pulse. It is a very rich source of proteins and carbohydrates.

INGREDIENTS

1. Gramflour — 100 gm
2. Onions (small, chopped) — 2
3. Carrot (small, chopped) — 1
4. Tomato (small, chopped) — 1
5. Capsicum (small) — 1
6. Soda bicarbonate — Pinch
7. Milk toned — ¼ cup
8. Green chillies (chopped) — 2
9. Coriander leaves — A few
10. Salt, cumin powder — To taste

METHOD

(1) Put gramflour and milk in a bowl. Mix salt, cumin powder and soda bicarbonate. Make a thick batter so that it is neither too thick nor too thin.
(2) Mix all the chopped vegetables and mix it thoroughly.
(3) Heat water in a shallow pan and keep it on low flame.
(4) Put this mixture with the help of a spoon gently and allow it to be cooked on low flame uncovered.
(5) Once it gets cooked, gently turn the side and allow it to be cooked from the other side also.
(6) Serve hot with green Dip or sauce.

GRAMFLOUR ROLLS

INGREDIENTS

1. Potatoes (boiled, mashed, medium sized) — 2
2. Peas (boiled) — ½ cup
3. Onion (chopped, small sized) — 2
4. Green chillies (chopped, small sized) — 2
5. Pomegranate seeds (Anardana) — ¼ tsp
6. Salt — To taste
7. Cumin powder — ¼ tsp
8. Coriander leaves — A few
9. Bread crumbs dry — 4-5 tsp
10. Gramflour — 1 cup

METHOD

(1) Mash the potatoes and mix peas, onion, chillies, coriander leaves together along with the masalas.
(2) Make a thick batter of Gramflour.
(3) Take the potato mixture and roll it into balls either round or oval.
(4) Dip these balls in the Gramflour mixture and keep it in the deep freezer for 5-7 minutes. Spread dry bread crumbs.
(5) Allow water to heat in a sauce pan, when the water starts boiling, put these rolls in it and cook them on low flame, turning them from side by side.
(6) Serve hot with Dip or garlic sauce.
(7) It can also be cooked in the microwave for **7-8 minutes** on **900 watt** either in the range or even in the grill.

GRAMFLOUR BREAD

INGREDIENTS

1.	Bread (medium sized)	2-3 slices
2.	Egg	1
3.	Onion (small, chopped)	2
4.	Green chillies (chopped)	2
5.	Coriander leaves	A few
6.	Gramflour	1 cup
7.	Salt, black pepper	To taste
8.	Cumin powder	¼ tsp

METHOD

(1) Break egg in a pan and add gramflour. Beat and mix thoroughly and allow it to set.

(2) Add salt, cumin powder and black pepper to the mixture.

(3) Take bread slices and dip them in the gramflour mixture.

(4) Keep them in a plate and set them in the freezer for 10 minutes.

(5) Heat water in a pan and allow the bread to be cooked only from one side.

(6) Serve hot with garnished onions, chopped chillies and coriander leaves.

NAVRATAN GRAMFLOUR

INGREDIENTS

1.	Gramflour	250gm
2.	Green chillies (chopped)	3-4
3.	Tomato (chopped) or tomato puree	5-6 tsp
4.	Grapes black (crushed)	10-12
5.	Cabbage (chopped)	Small cup
6.	Eggplants & carrots (chopped, small)	2
7.	Salt	To taste
8.	Soda bicarbonate	Pinch
9.	Cumin powder	¼ tsp
10.	Milk	¼ cup

METHOD

(1) Make a batter of gramflour with milk and soda bicarbonate.

(2) Put this batter in a tray or a plate and then keep it in the refrigerator for 5-7 minutes.

(3) Make cuts in the layer of gramflour with a knife and then put all the chopped ingredients one by one on the gramflour; so that a rainbow of different colours is formed.

(4) Sprinkle salt and cumin powder over it. Cover it with a cellophane paper.

(5) Keep it in the microwave and heat it for 8-10 minutes till it gets cooked.

(6) Serve hot with coconut Dip.

GRAMFLOUR NUTS

INGREDIENTS

1. Almonds — 5-6
2. Cashew nuts — 8-10
3. Dates — 2-3
4. Peanuts — 50 gm
5. Salt and chat masala — To taste
6. Pistachio — 6-7
7. Kishmish — 10-15
8. Gramflour — ½ cup
9. Water — For batter

METHOD

(1) Soak all the nuts overnight so that they can be consumed even by the cardiac or hypertensive patients.

(2) Make a thin batter of gramflour, add salt to it.

(3) Roast all the nuts together for 5-8 minutes in the microwave oven till they become light brown.

(4) Put all the nuts in the gramflour and again heat them in the oven for 10-15 minutes.

(5) Sprinkle chat masala on it and serve it hot with tea or coffee.

GRAMFLOUR PAKORAS

INGREDIENTS

1.	Gramflour	250 gm
2.	Potato (sliced)	6-10
3.	Cauliflower (florets)	5-6
4.	Cheese slices	4-5
5.	Soda bicarbonate	Pinch
6.	Chat masala	To taste
7.	Red chilly powder	To taste
8.	Sauce	To serve

METHOD

(1) Wash florets of cauliflower and sprinkle salt and red chilly on them.

(2) Cut cheese into two and sprinkle the layer of chat masala on it.

(3) Make a batter of gramflour, add soda bicarbonate and dip the vegetables in the batter and heat them in the oven for 10-12 minutes by turning sides one by one.

(4) Sprinkle chat masala and serve hot with tomato sauce.

VEGETABLE UPMA

INGREDIENTS

1. Semolina (Semolina) — 1 cup
2. Peas (steamed) — ¼ cup
3. Carrot (grated) — ¼ cup
4. Onions (chopped) — ¼ cup
5. Mustard seeds — ¼ tsp
6. Curry leaves — 4-5
7. Chickpea pulse — ½ tsp
8. Urad pulse — ½ tsp
9. Salt — To taste
10. Coriander leaves — 2 tsp
11. Red chilly powder — ¼ tsp

METHOD

(1) Dry roast the semolina lightly and keep it aside.

(2) Now roast the mustard seeds, curry leaves, chickpea pulse, urad pulse and onion one by one.

(3) To the roasted masala, add salt, steamed peas, grated carrot and roasted semolina.

(4) Then add water and cook them until they are cooked.

(5) Serve with coriander mint Dip.

VEGETABLE SEEKH KABAB

INGREDIENTS

1.	Potato (medium sized)	1
2.	Brown bread	1 piece
3.	Cottage cheese (grated)	1 tsp
4.	Ginger	1 piece
5.	Green chilly	1/2
6.	Coriander leaves	A few
7.	Garlic	2 cloves
8.	Salt	To taste
9.	Dried mango powder	¼ tsp
10.	Cumin powder (roasted)	¼ tsp
11.	Red chilly powder	¼ tsp

METHOD

(1) Boil, peel and mash the potato.

(2) Grind ginger, green chillies and coriander leaves together.

(3) Add to this paste, grated cottage cheese, seasonings and soaked bread slice. Add mashed potato to it and mix well.

(4) Divide this mixture into 3 portions and flatten them. Using a wet hand fold this mixture thoroughly.

(5) Grill till it becomes golden brown in colour.

(6) Garnish with grated cheese/cabbage or lettuce leaves.

(7) Serve hot with Dip.

VEG. SHAMMI KABABS

INGREDIENTS

1. Nutrela granules — 1 cup
2. Bread — 1½ slices
3. Onions (chopped) — ½ cup
4. Green chillies (chopped) — 2-3
5. Ginger garlic paste — 1 tsp
6. Black pepper powder — ½ tsp
7. Salt — To taste
8. Red chilly powder — To taste
9. Ajinomoto — A pinch

METHOD

(1) Boil the granules, drain and mash them in the mixer.

(2) Crumble the bread and use it as a binder.

(3) Add chopped onions, green chillies, garlic ginger paste, salt and black pepper.

(4) Make round balls and bake them at 280°for 15 minutes.

(5) When crisp, serve hot with Dip.

VEG. PANCAKE

INGREDIENTS

1. Potato (medium sized) — 1
2. Cauliflower florets — 5-6
3. Carrot — 1
4. Peas (shelled) — ¼ cup
5. Tomato — 1
6. Tomato sauce — 1 tsp
7. Salt — To taste
8. Chilly power — To taste
9. Pancake batter — 1 basic recipe

METHOD

(1) Cut the potato into small pieces and the carrot into long shreds.

(2) Put the vegetables and seasonings in a pan, cover and cook them on slow heat.

(3) Add tomato sauce when it is cooked.

(4) Spread some vegetable filling on one pancake and cover it with the second pancake. Again put the filling and cover it with the third pancake.

(5) Garnish with tomato slice and serve.

VEG. NOODLES

INGREDIENTS

1.	Noodles	1 cup
2.	French beans	½ cup
3.	Carrot	½ cup
4.	Cabbage	½ cup
5.	Capsicum	½ cup
6.	Spring onion (sliced)	¼ cup
7.	Garlic (chopped)	2-3 cloves
8.	Salt	To taste
9.	White pepper powder	¼ tsp
10.	Soya sauce	2 tsp
11.	Chilly sauce	½ tsp
12.	Ajinomoto	¼ tsp

METHOD

(1) Boil noodles in plenty of salted water. Then, drain it in a sieve, pour cold water over it and keep it aside.

(2) Shred the cabbage and carrots, finely chop the capsicum and French beans.

(3) To a pan add garlic and sliced onion, sauté them.

(4) Then add French beans, carrot, salt, pepper, and Ajinomoto to it. Cool them for 5 minutes.

(5) Add vegetables and again cook for 5-7 minutes.

(6) Finally add noodles along with soya sauce and chilly sauce. Mix them well.

(7) Serve hot.

UPMA

INGREDIENTS

1. Semolina — 1 cup
2. Mustard seeds — 1 tsp
3. Black gram pulse — 2 tsp
4. Bengal gram pulse — 2 tsp
5. Green chillies — 2-3
6. Ginger — 1 piece
7. Curry leaves — A few
8. Coriander leaves — Few
9. Onion (chopped) — 1
10. Salt — To taste

METHOD

(1) Dry roast 1 cup of semolina.

(2) In a pan, add mustard seeds, black gram pulse, Bengal gram pulse, green chillies, ginger, curry leaves and sauté them till they are cooked.

(3) Add chopped onions to it and sauté till they become golden brown.

(4) Now add 3-4 cups of water and salt to taste.

(5) When water starts boiling, add Semolina and stir it till it is cooked.

(6) Garnish with coriander leaves and serve hot with either garlic or mint Dip.

STUFFED EGG WHITES

INGREDIENTS

1. Eggs (boiled) — 2
2. Cottage cheese (grated) — 1 tsp
3. Peas — 2 tsp
4. Tomato ketchup — 1 tsp
5. Salt, red chilly powder — To taste
6. Turmeric — ¼ tsp

METHOD

(1) Hard boil the eggs. Then cool and shell them.

(2) Cut them into halves and remove the yolk.

(3) To the grated cottage cheese, add seasonings and steamed peas and cook on slow flame.

(4) Remove from heat, add tomato ketchup and mix it well.

(5) Put this filling into the egg white and serve with salad.

STEAMED CABBAGE ROLLS

INGREDIENTS

1.	Cabbage leaves (washed)	6-7 leaves
2.	Potatoes (boiled, medium sized)	4-5
3.	Onion (finely chopped)	1 big
4.	Garlic	4-5 clove
5.	Coriander leaves	A few
6.	Green chillies (chopped)	2
7.	Salt and pepper	To taste

METHOD

(1) Mix potato, onion, garlic, coriander leaves, chillies, salt and pepper together.

(2) Stuff this mixture in each cabbage leaf. Put a tooth pick on the fold to hold the mixture in.

(3) Keep each roll for steaming in a pressure cooker or a steamer.

(4) Steam for 10 minutes.

(5) To make it little crisp, toast it either in an oven or microwave till it gets brown.

(6) Serve hot with Dip.

CUTLETS

INGREDIENTS

1.	Potato (boiled)	2-3
2.	Chickpea pulse (soaked)	1 tsp
3.	Green chilly	1/2
4.	Spinach (chopped)	1 cup
5.	Coriander leaves	A few
6.	Salt	To taste
7.	Mango powder	¼ tsp
8.	Garam masala	¼ tsp
9.	Red chilly powder	¼ tsp
10.	Bread crumbs	2 tsp

METHOD

(1) Boil, peel and mash the potatoes.
(2) Cook chickpea pulse till tender and drain off the excess water.
(3) Wash and chop the spinach, green chilly and coriander leaves.
(4) Mix all the above ingredients along with the spices.
(5) Shape into cutlets of desired shape and coat with bread crumbs.
(6) Bake them in the oven till they turned golden brown.
(7) Garnish with grated cabbage.
(8) Serve with Dip.

Note: Garam Masala: corinander seeds, cumin seeds, black pepper corns, black cumin seeds, dry ginger powder, cardamom, cloves, cinnamon.

SPICY SPINACH BALLS

INGREDIENTS

1.	Spinach (finely chopped)	2 cups
2.	Green chilly (chopped)	1
3.	Gramflour	1 tsp
4.	Wheat flour	2 tsp
5.	Curd	2 tsp
6.	Asafetida (Heeng)	A pinch
7.	Red chilly powder	½ tsp
8.	Sugar	Pinch
9.	Salt	To taste

METHOD

(1) Mix all the ingredients together.

(2) If the mixture is too dry to shape into balls, add curd.

(3) Now shape them into balls and steam them in a pressure cooker.

(4) Serve hot with Dip.

IDLI

INGREDIENTS

1.	Semolina	2 cups
2.	Green chillies	4-5
3.	Ginger	1 piece
4.	Salt	1 tsp
5.	Sour curd	1 cup
6.	Mustard seeds	1 tsp
7.	Carrots (grated)	½ cup
8.	Coriander leaves	To garnish

METHOD

(1) Dry roast 2 cups of Semolina in a pan. Keep it aside.

(2) In the same pan add mustard seeds. When they sparkle, add green chillies and ginger.

(3) Mix all these with 1 cup of curd and 1 tsp of salt. Add Semolina to it.

(4) In the idli steamer, add grated carrot and chopped coriander leaves. Pour the prepared mixture.

(5) Add enough water to the mixture only at the time of pouring into the boiling trays to prevent it from sticking.

(6) Serve hot with mint or coconut Dip.

ROASTED CHICKPEA BRITTLE

INGREDIENTS

1. Roasted chickpea/puffed rice   ½ cup
2. Jaggery   1 cup

METHOD

(1) Grind the chickpeas coarsely. If you are using puffed rice then lightly roast them.

(2) Crush jaggery and cook with water (2 tsp) till it becomes hard.

(3) To this add Chickpea/puffed rice.

(4) Put this mixture on butter paper and roll into ¼" thickness.

(5) While hot, cut it with a knife.

(6) When it becomes cool, break it into pieces along with cut marks.

(7) Serve it.

RICE MOONG PULSE IDLI

INGREDIENTS

1.	Moong pulse	½ cup
2.	Rice	½ cup
3.	Soda bicarbonate	1 pinch
4.	Salt	To taste
5.	Fenugreek seeds	¼ tsp

METHOD

(1) Soak rice, pulse and fenugreek seeds in water for 5-6 hours.

(2) Then grind the ingredients and leave them overnight.

(3) Now add soda bicarbonate and salt, put it into the idli stand for steaming.

(4) Serve hot with Dip or sambhar.

PANCAKE

INGREDIENTS

1. Flour — ¾ cup
2. Milk — ½ cup
3. Egg white — 1
4. Salt — To taste

METHOD

(1) Sift the flour along with salt in a bowl.

(2) Make a well in the centre of flour and put the egg white into it.

(3) Gradually add milk, mix and beat it thoroughly till the batter is smooth and free of lumps.

(4) Allow the batter to stand in a cool place for ½ hour. Give a final whisk before using.

(5) Put this batter in a pan and spread it evenly. Cook in one side till it gets brown.

(6) Prepare all the pancakes in the same manner.

VERMICELLI

INGREDIENTS

1. Rice — 4 cups
2. Water — 4 cups
3. Salt — To taste

METHOD

(1) Wash 4 cups of rice well. Soak and wash them again. Drain and pound it into flour.
(2) Sift in through a fine sieve. Dry well. Add 2 tsp of salt.
(3) For each leveled cup of dried flour, use 1 cup of water.
(4) Measure and pour water in a wide mouthed vessel. Add salt and boil.
(5) When the water starts boiling vigorously, add flour to it and keep on stirring with a ladle to prevent the formation of lumps.
(6) Cook for 5 minutes, till the bright white colour becomes dull.
(7) Remove from fire. Keep it covered for about 10 minutes till the water condenses and drips from the plate, covering the vessel.
(8) Empty the cooked flour on to a plate. Dip the hand in water and knead the flour well.
(9) Pinch and roll the flour into balls of a size suited to the Vermicelli maker.
(10) Boil water separately, when it starts boiling put the flour balls into it.
(11) When almost cooked, flour balls will start floating.
(12) Take out the balls from the water. Put it in the Vermicelli maker. Press it out through the Vermicelli maker.
(13) Spread it on a plate. Repeat with each ball.
(14) Cool the Vermicelli. After cooling, take as much Vermicelli as is needed to prepare the different kinds of Vermicelli.

PEPPER VERMICELLI

INGREDIENTS

1.	Pepper	1 tsp
2.	Cumin seeds	1 tsp
3.	Green chillies	2-3
4.	Mustard seeds	1 tsp
5.	Bengal gram pulse	1 tsp
6.	Salt	To taste

METHOD

(1) Heat a pan.

(2) Put some mustard seeds, when they pop, add pepper, cumin seeds and salt.

(3) Now add green chillies and curry leaves.

(4) To this add cooled Vermicelli and mix them well.

(5) Serve hot.

PAO BHAJI

INGREDIENTS

Pao (a type of circular bread)	8-10
For Bhaji	
1. Potatoes (boiled)	1
2. Peas (boiled)	½ cup
3. Onion (chopped, small sized)	1
4. Capsicum (chopped)	2
5. French beans (boiled)	½ cup
6. Coriander leaves	Few
7. Tomatoes (finely chopped)	3
8. Jimikand	1 cup
9. Ginger garlic paste	1 tsp
10. Salt	To taste
11. Red chilly powder	1 tsp
12. Turmeric powder	½ tsp
13. Pao bhaji masala	2 tsp

METHOD

(1) Sauté the onion and tomatoes in a dry pan.
(2) Add boiled vegetables along with masalas to them except pao bhaji masala.
(3) Cook till all the vegetables are well mashed and have blended with the masala. Now put the pao bhaji masala and again mix them well.
(4) Cut the bun (pao) into halves and toast them on a tava.
(5) Serve the pao with bhaji garnished with coriander leaves.

MOONG PULSE DHOKLA

INGREDIENTS

1. Moong (green gram with skin) — 1 cup
2. Gramflour — 2 tsp
3. Fresh curd — 1 tsp
4. Asafetida (Heeng) (dissolved in little water) — Pinch
5. Salt and green chillies — To taste

METHOD

(1) Soak pulse for at least 2 hours. Drain and keep it aside.
(2) Add to it green chillies and grind them. Add water only if required.
(3) Add g]ramflour, curd, asafetida and salt to the batter.
(4) Pour a thin layer of this batter into a steel plate and sprinkle cabbage on it.
(5) Steam it in the cooker for 5-7 minutes.
(6) Serve hot with tamarind Dip.

DAHI VADA

INGREDIENTS

1.	Moong pulse (with skin)	½ cup
2.	Fresh curd	1 tsp
3.	Asafetida (Heeng)	A pinch
4.	Green chillies	2-3
5.	Cumin powder	¼ tsp
6.	Chilly powder	¼ tsp
7.	Soda bicarbonate	½ tsp
8.	Salt	To taste
9.	Coriander leaves	1 tsp

METHOD

(1) Soak the pulse for at least 3-4 hours. Drain and keep it aside.
(2) Add green chillies to it and blend it in a mixer, adding little water.
(3) Add asafetida and soda bicarbonate to this batter.
(4) Heat a nonstick toaster and spread 1 tsp of this mixture in each cavity. Close it and heat.
(5) The mixture is toasted into small triangular pieces. Then take out the pieces from the toaster.
(6) Dip them in water for 5 minutes, squeeze the water and arrange on the serving dish.
(7) Beat the curd along with water and salt.
(8) Add green chillies, chilly and cumin powder to it.
(9) Serve.

BURGERS

INGREDIENTS

Burger buns	1
For Cutlets	
1. Potato (boiled, peeled and mashed)	1
2. Green peas (shelled)	2 tsp
3. Carrot (shredded)	1
4. Onion (chopped)	1
5. Chilly powder	½ tsp
6. Garam masala	To taste
7. Vinegar	1 tsp
8. Salt and pepper	To taste

METHOD

(1) In a dry pan, sauté the onions till they become light brown.
(2) Add peas and carrot to them. Keep on stirring over low heat till the moisture dries.
(3) Now add salt, pepper, chilly powder and garam masala to it. Stir well.
(4) Finally add the mashed potatoes and vinegar, mix well. Remove from heat and keep it aside.
(5) When it becomes cool, divide this mixture into 2 portions and roll it into balls, flatten them slightly between the palms. Bake them in the oven till they get brownish.
(6) Slice the burger bun horizontally. Place the cutlet inside and close the bun.
(7) Serve hot with tomato sauce.

Note: Garam Masala: corinander seeds, cumin seeds, black pepper corns, black cumin seeds, dry ginger powder, cardamom, cloves, cinnamon.

LEMON VERMICELLI

INGREDIENTS

1.	Lemon	2
2.	Bengal gram pulse	1 tsp
3.	Mustard seeds	1 tsp
4.	Red chillies	3-4
5.	Green chillies	4-5
6.	Asafetida (Heeng)	A pinch
7.	Turmeric powder	¼ tsp
8.	Salt	¼ tsp

METHOD

(1) Soak the Bengal gram pulse in a pan.

(2) Squeeze and strain the juice of lemons and keep it aside.

(3) Add turmeric powder.

(4) Dry roast the seasonings and add salt to it.

(5) To this add green chillies. Now add pulse to it and further sauté it. If it is dry sprinkle water to avoid it sticking to the sides of a pan.

(6) Now add lemon juice.

(7) Mix all this together to cool Vermicelli and serve.

DOSA

INGREDIENTS

1. Parboiled rice — 2 cups
2. Red gram pulse — 1 cup
3. Fenugreek seeds — 1½ tsp
4. Salt — To taste

METHOD

(1) Soak the rice and pulse separately with fenugreek seeds overnight.

(2) Grind the rice to a rough paste and the pulse and fenugreek seeds to a soft spongy mass.

(3) Mix all these together with desired amount of salt and again soak it overnight.

(4) Next day, cut an onion into half and run it on the pan over which the dosa is to be prepared.

(5) Pour a little batter over the pan. If the batter is too thick, add a little water for the desired consistency.

(6) Serve hot with coconut Dip.

BAKED SAMOSA

INGREDIENTS

1. Flour — 1 cup
2. Salt — To taste

For filling:

1. Cabbage, peas (shredded) — 50 g
2. Onions (finely chopped) — 2
3. Green chillies, ginger paste — 1 tsp
4. Lemon juice — 1 lemon

METHOD

DOUGH:

1. Mix the white flour and salt and knead with enough water to make soft dough.
2. Roll out thin chapattis.
3. Roast the chapattis on one side till done.

TO FILL:

1. Sprinkle a pinch of salt on cabbage/peas and keep so for 10 minutes.
2. Then squeeze out any extra water.
3. Mix rest of the ingredients with the cabbage.
4. Cut each chapati into half and make a cone of each half.
5. Now fill the ingredients into the cone. Close each cone and use a toothpick to hold the folds together.
6. Put it into the oven and bake on both the sides.
7. Serve hot with Dip.

BAKED PURIS

INGREDIENTS

1. Wheat flour — 1 cup
2. White flour — ½ cup
3. Salt — To taste
4. Coriander leaves — A few
5. Mint leaves — A few

METHOD

(1) Mix all the ingredients together and knead with enough water to make a little hard dough.
(2) Roll out thin puris and prick each with a fork.
(3) Keep these puris in the baking tray greased with a teaspoon of curd.
(4) Heat the oven to 200°C and roast the puris for 10 minutes.
(5) Serve hot with potato bhaji or green Dip.

BHEL PURI

INGREDIENTS

1.	Chickpea pulse	¾ cup
2.	Ginger (small piece)	1
3.	Green chillies	1-2
4.	Onion (small, chopped)	¼ cup
5.	Garlic cloves	2
6.	Mustard seeds	½ tsp
7.	Sour curd	¾ tsp
8.	Lemon juice	½-1 tsp
9.	Sugar	½-1 tsp
10.	Asafetida (Heeng)	A pinch
11.	Black pepper	¼ tsp
12.	Curry leaves	6-7
13.	Salt	To taste
14.	Turmeric	A pinch
15.	Coriander leaves (chopped)	A few
16.	Soda bicarbonate	¼ tsp

METHOD

(1) Soak the chickpea pulse overnight. Drain the water in the morning.
(2) Take ½ of the pulse, to this add ginger, green chillies, curd and grind it coarsely.
(3) To this mixture add the remaining whole pulse along with salt and turmeric powder. Keep it covered for 4-5 hours.
(4) Add lemon juice, soda bicarbonate and sugar to the mixture.
(5) Put this mixture on idli steamer and steam it.
(6) When cooked, cool it and crumble it.
(7) To this add little asafetida and mustard powder. Heat it.
(8) In a pan, sauté garlic and onion till it is golden brown. To this add curry leaves and mix it to the crumbled mixture.
(9) Garnish with coriander leaves and serve with Dip.

CHIDWA

INGREDIENTS

1. Chidwa (beaten rice with pea nuts) — 50 g
2. Onion (small, chopped) — 1
3. Potato (small, boiled, cut into pieces) — 1
4. Peas (boiled) — ½ cup
5. Green chillies — 2
6. Salt — To taste
7. Turmeric powder — ¼ tsp
8. Black pepper — Pinch

METHOD

(1) Wash and soak chidwa in water for 10-12 minutes. Keep it aside.

(2) Heat water in a pan, add onions and cook till they become brown. Now add potato, peas and green chillies to it.

(3) To this add salt, turmeric and black pepper. Whet it gets cooked put chidwa and mix them together well.

(4) Serve with green Dip.

CANOPY

INGREDIENTS

1.	Canopies (Lachha Tokri)	5-6
2.	Potato (small, boiled)	1
3.	Peas (boiled)	½ cup
4.	Cottage cheese	50 g
5.	Onion (chopped)	1
6.	Salt	To taste
7.	Sprouts	½ cup
8.	Black pepper	¼ tsp
9.	Tomato sauce	

METHOD

(1) Heat the canopies in the microwave for 5-8 minutes.

(2) Arrange them in the tray.

(3) Mix potatoes and peas and add salt and black pepper to them.

(4) Fill the canopies with different fillings of potato, peas, cheese, sprouts, seasoned with tomato sauce.

KACHORI

INGREDIENTS

1. Flour	250 gm
2. Curd	100 gm
3. Salt	Pinch
4. Fenugreek leaves (kasoori methi)	¼ tsp

For Filling:

1. Peas (Boiled)	100 gm
2. Red chilly powder	½ tsp

METHOD

(1) Mix flour, curd and salt. Add water to make a soft dough of flour mix.
(2) Add boiled peas to fenugreek leaves & chilly so that the material for filling is ready.
(3) Make small balls of flour & press to make holes in them. Fill them with peas and close them from the top to make a round ball.
(4) Grease the non-stick platter and put the balls on low flame for 10 min.
(5) Once they turn brown reverse them.
(6) The kachori is ready to be served with either potato curry or any dip.

NOTE: Instead of matar, filling can be of cheese or onion or dry masala (like salt, chilly, cumin, garam masala)

Snacks

TOFU PAKORAS

INGREDIENTS

1. Tofu — 200 gm
2. Flour — 100 gm
3. Fenugreek leaves — ¼ tsp
4. Black salt — ¼ tsp

METHOD

(1) Dilute flour with water and make a batter. Add Fenugreek leaves and black salt to it.

(2) Keep a pan on low flame and add few drops of water. Let it steam for few minutes.

(3) Cut tofu in small pieces, soak in flour solution. Cook it on low flame for 15-20 minutes.

(4) Once it turns brown, turn it with a knife and cook it on both sides.

(5) Seve hot with tomato sauce or Dip.

MIXED VEG PAKORAS

INGREDIENTS

1.	Finely cut & chopped veggies (Onion, carrot, cauliflower)	50 gm each
2.	Flour	150 gm
3.	Fenugreek leaves	¼ tsp
4.	Green chilly (Chopped)	2-3
5.	Black salt	¼ tsp

METHOD

(1) Mix water and make a thin batter of flour, add Fenugreek leaves, black salt and chopped veggies with green chillies.

(2) Allow it to remain so for 10 minutes.

(3) Let the ingredients mix together. Then make small balls of the mixture.

(4) Grease the platter dish with one drop of oil and add the mixture.

(5) Keep it on low flame for 10-15 minutes. Once it turns brown turn it on the other side.

(6) Again turn it and once it become crispy, turn off the flame.

(7) Serve hot with garlic or green Dip.

BABY CORN PAKORAS

INGREDIENTS

1. Baby Corns — 10-12
2. Flour — 50 gm
3. Oregano — Pinch
4. Milk — 30 ml
5. Black salt — ¼ tsp
6. Fenugreek leaves — ¼ tsp

METHOD

(1) Keep nonstick pan on low flame. Put 2-3 tsps of water.

(2) Allow it to heat for 5 minutes.

(3) Make a thin batter of flour. Add oregano, Fenugreek leaves, milk and black salt to it.

(4) Wash baby corns and dip them in the batter.

(5) Keep it on low flame in the nonstick pan. Allow it to be there for 15-20 minutes. Turn the baby corns when they become brown. Allow them to be crispy.

(6) Serve hot with mint dip.

CHATPATE CORNS

INGREDIENTS

1.	Corns	200 gm
2.	Green chilly (chopped)	2
3.	Garlic (chopped)	2 slices
4.	Cumin (whole)	1 tsp
5.	Black salt	¼ tsp
6.	Lemon juice	1 tsp
7.	Mango powder	¼ tsp

METHOD

(1) Take a bowl and mix all the ingredients except corns.

(2) Steam corns in a closed pan for 5-7 minutes.

(3) Mix the ingredients with corns and warm in the microwave for 30 seconds.

(4) Luring corns ready to eat.

ARVI LEAF PAKORA

INGREDIENTS

1.	Arvi Leaves (colocasia)	5-6
2.	Flour	100 gm
3.	Ajwain	Pinch
4.	Black salt	¼ tsp
5.	Red chilly flakes	¼ tsp
6.	Toothpick (to lock the roll)	5-6

METHOD

(1) Soak the leaves of arvi (colocasia) in water for 10 minutes so that the aroma is washed off.

(2) Make a thin batter of flour with water.

(3) Take out the leaves and mix chilly flakes, ajwain, and black salt together.

(4) Sprinkle them on the leaves, make a roll of leaf and lock them with toothpick.

(5) Heat a nonstick pan on low flame. Put few tablespoon of water in it. Dip the leaves into the batter and keep them on low flame. When one side turns brown, turn on the other side.

(6) Allow them to be cooked on both sides.

(7) Serve them hot with Dip or sauce.

CRISPY PINEAPPLE

INGREDIENTS

1. Pineapple (cut)	1
2. Black salt	Pinch
3. Lemon juice	1 tsp
4. Flour	20-30 gm

METHOD

(1) Keep a nonstick pan on low flame. Once it is hot, put 2-3 tsp of water.

(2) Make a thin batter of flour and dip pineapple pieces in it.

(3) Cook it on low flame for 10-12 minutes.

(4) Once it is done from one side sprinkle black salt and lemon juice over it.

(5) Serve it hot as a wonderful snacky fruit.

part 9
VEGETABLES

Vegetables are nature's best gift. All the vegetables, right from stems to roots to tubers to bulbs which include colocasia, beetroot, potatoes, onions etc. are available to humanity for consumption. Every vegetable has its own taste, nutrients and advantages. Let us have a look at these vegetables one by one and the varying recipes that can be made using them which adds an exotic flavour and style to our menu.

- Potato Dum
- Cumin with Potato
- Garlic with Potato
- Potato with Masala
- Potato Fenugreek/Chenopodium/Spinach
- Potato with Peas
- Potato Potato with Paneer
- Potato with Cauliflower
- Potato Kofta
- Onion with Peas
- Onion with Mushroom
- Soya with Onion
- Onion with Capsicum
- Stuffed Tomatoes
- Tomato Curry
- Tomato Cheese
- Cauliflower Masala
- Cauliflower with Potato
- Cauliflower with Peas
- Cauliflower Korma
- Peas with Potato
- Peas Paneer
- Peas Mushroom
- Carrot Peas
- Carrot with Potato
- Carrot Katar
- Cabbage with Cheese
- Cabbage with Peas
- Cabbage with Mushrooms
- Beans with Potato
- Sweet Pumpkin
- Bitter Gourd
- Bitter Gourd Chopped
- Stuffed Lady Finger
- Chopped Lady Finger
- Eggplant Bhartha
- Potato with Eggplant
- Eggplant with Colocasia

- Colocasia with Onion
- Vegetable Curry
- Capsicum with Potato
- Capsicum Paneer
- Grated Radish
- Radish with Potato
- Nutty Mutty Ginger
- Floating Spring Onions
- Sweet 'n' Sour Jugnu
- Heeng-E-Matar
- Malai Kofta
- Beetroot
- Nutty Mutty Radish
- Lotus Stem with Cheese

POTATO

Potato is the commonest modified root available in the Indian kitchen and cuisine as well. It is a vegetable that grows under the ground and is consumed as a whole. It can be boiled, baked, roasted or even deep fried. It is used as such or along with other vegetables as a combined partner. It is available in different sizes and shapes. But for good cooking the potatoes should be of uniform size. It is a rich source of carbohydrates, starch and vitamin. Let us have a look at the different varieties of potato preparations.

POTATO DUM

INGREDIENTS

1.	Potatoes (medium sized, boiled)	8-10
2.	Tomatoes and ginger (grind to paste)	4-5
3.	Garlic flakes	2-3
4.	Salt, black pepper	To taste
5.	Cumin powder	¼ tsp
6.	Black salt	To taste
7.	Mango powder	¼ tsp
8.	Chat masala	¼ tsp
9.	Curd	½ cup

METHOD

(1) Put curd in a dish and churn it. Take half of it and mix salt, cumin powder, black salt, black pepper and chat masala in it. Put all the potatoes and mix them in the curd thoroughly. Keep them in the cool unit of refrigerator for 10 min.

(2) Heat water in a saucepan. Once it starts boiling, put garlic flakes in it and crush it gently till it starts giving its odour. Put the tomato, ginger paste and allow it to heat in low flame till it become thick.

(3) Add curd and mango powder and heat it further till it becomes quite thick.

(4) Now put the cool potatoes in the pan and cook it for 8-10 minutes more.

(5) While in the pan, make small holes in the potatoes with the help of fork and sprinkle cumin powder on them.

(6) Serve hot.

CUMIN WITH POTATO

INGREDIENTS

1. Potatoes (medium size, cut into small pieces) — 2-3
2. Mustard seeds — Few
3. Cumin seeds — Few
4. Salt — To taste
5. Turmeric — ¼ tsp
6. Soya sauce — ¼ tsp
7. Green chillies — 2-3

METHOD

(1) Heat water in a saucepan and put cumin seeds and mustard seeds into it.

(2) When they start crackling, add soya sauce, green chillies and turmeric powder. Heat it for 2-3 minutes.

(3) Then, put cut pieces of potatoes and mix it thoroughly. Keep it on low flame. When they start getting cooked, put salt on them. Allow it to cook for 20-30 minutes on low flame.

(4) Serve hot.

GARLIC WITH POTATO

INGREDIENTS

1. Potatoes (chopped small) — 4-5
2. Garlic flakes — 8-10
3. Green chillies (cut finely) — 2-3
4. Salt — To taste
5. Black pepper — To taste

METHOD

(1) Heat water in a saucepan. Put garlic flakes and cook them for 5-10 minutes.

(2) Put green chillies and salt into it and heat it for 5-6 minutes.

(3) Now add potatoes and cook it for 15-20 minutes. When they start boiling, add either milk or water.

(4) When cooked, sprinkle black pepper on the potatoes and serve hot.

POTATO MASALA

INGREDIENTS

1.	Potatoes (boiled, cut into small pieces)	5-6
2.	Cloves	4-5
3.	Big cardamom	1
4.	Coriander powder	1 tsp
5.	Custard powder	1 tsp
6.	Salt, black pepper, cumin powder	To taste
7.	Curry leaves	1-2
8.	Green chillies (cut into long pieces)	2-3

METHOD

(1) Mix all the ingredients (dry masalas) and ground them to a powder.

(2) Make a thin paste of custard powder with water.

(3) Take a pan, put the custard powder batter and potatoes in it. Sprinkle the dry masala and salt over it.

(4) Heat it either in a microwave oven for 10 minutes or on low flame for 10 minutes.

(5) Serve hot either as a snack or a vegetable.

POTATO WITH FENUGREEK/ CHENOPODIUM/SPINACH

INGREDIENTS

1. Potatoes (boiled or raw cut into pieces) — 4-5
2. Chenopodium/fenugreek/spinach leaves (washed and chopped) — 250 gm
3. Green chillies (chopped) — 2
4. Salt, black pepper, cumin powder — To Taste

METHOD

(1) Heat water in a pan, put cumin powder, green chillies and salt into it.

(2) Heat them for 1-2 minutes. Add the potatoes and cook them for 5-10 minutes till they become soft. Add salt.

(3) Now add chopped methi or chenopodium or spinach leaves to it. Mix them thoroughly and cover the pan. Keep on low flame for 8-10 minutes.

(4) Serve hot with maize flour or millet flour Indian bread.

POTATO WITH PEAS

INGREDIENTS

1. Peas (shelled) — 50 g
2. Potatoes (raw or boiled cut into pieces, medium sized) — 2-3
3. Ginger, garlic, tomatoes, onion, and green chillies (ground to a fine paste) — 1-2
4. Salt — To taste
5. Turmeric — To taste
6. Coriander powder — ¼ tsp
7. Chat masala — To taste

METHOD

(1) Heat water in a saucepan. Put the masala (paste) and heat it on low flame. Cook it thoroughly till it starts giving the flavour.

(2) Add salt, coriander powder and potatoes. Cook it for some time.

(3) When potatoes are soft, put green peas and add water to make a gravy. Heat on low flame. When tender, sprinkle chat masala and serve hot.

POTATO WITH PANEER

INGREDIENTS

1.	Potatoes (cut into pieces)	2-3
2.	Paneer cubes	10-15
3.	Masala (paste onion, garlic, tomatoes, green chilly)	
4.	Cloves	1-2
5.	Salt	To taste
6.	Coriander powder	¼ tsp
7.	Turmeric powder	¼ tsp
8.	Coriander leaves	A few

METHOD

(1) Heat water in a coriander pan. Cook masala for 15-20 minutes, add cloves, coriander powder and turmeric.

(2) Put potatoes and allow it to cook for 15-20 minutes.

(3) Add paneer cubes and water to make thick gravy.

(4) When it becomes thick, add salt and garnish with coriander leaves.

POTATO WITH CAULIFLOWER

INGREDIENTS

1.	Potatoes (cubical shape)	5-6
2.	Florets of cauliflower	200 g
3.	Masala	3-4 tsp
4.	Salt	To taste
5.	Coriander powder	¼ tsp
6.	Black pepper	Pinch
7.	Turmeric powder	¼ tsp

METHOD

a. Heat water in a pan. Cook masala for 15-20 minutes, add cloves, coriander powder and turmeric.

b. Put potatoes and florets of cauliflower and cook it for 15-20 minutes.

c. When it cooked, add salt and garnish with coriander leaves.

NOTE: To make any preparation with potatoes as a vegetable combination, basic masala, wet and dry, remains the same except the vegetable to be combined.

POTATO KOFTA

INGREDIENTS

1.	Potato (small, grated)	1
2.	Green chillies (chopped)	2
3.	Salt	To taste
4.	Soda bicarbonate	Pinch
5.	Masala (as per instructions)	
6.	Turmeric powder	¼ tsp
7.	Cumin powder	¼ tsp
8.	Gramflour	4-5 tsp

METHOD

(1) Grate potatoes and mix gramflour, soda bicarbonate, salt and green chillies.

(2) Make a thick paste and roll them into balls.

(3) Heat these balls in the oven or steam them in an open sauce pan.

(4) Heat water in a sauce pan, add masala, and cook it for 20-25 minutes. Add cumin, turmeric powder and salt. Make a hick gravy.

(5) Heat water in a pan and keep the formed balls in the warm water for 5-7 minutes. Press them softly between the palms and add it to the gravy mixture.

(6) Cook it for 5 minutes and serve hot.

ONION

It is also one of the commonest and frequently used vegetables. It is used not only as a base for all the vegetables, pulses and even cereal preparations but as an entitled vegetable also. It is a modified root with many layers. It has a good strong medicinal value too. It helps in lowering high blood pressure, reduces cholesterol and helps in thinning the blood. It reduces acidity and helps in relieving muscle pains. Let us have a look on the recipes made using it.

ONION WITH PEAS

INGREDIENTS

1. Onion (small size) — 5-6
2. Peas (boiled) — ½ cup
3. Masala — 2-3 tsp
4. Salt, black pepper — To taste
5. Milk — ¼ cup

METHOD

(1) Heat water in a pan and add masala to it. Cook it on low flame for 15-20 minutes. Add salt, black pepper, onions (peeled) and boiled peas.
(2) Mix it thoroughly and heat them on low flame.
(3) When the mixture gets thick, add milk and heat for 2-3 minutes.
(4) Serve hot.

ONION WITH MUSHROOM

INGREDIENTS

1.	Onions (small)	5-6
2.	Mushroom (full)	100 g
3.	Masala	¼ cup
4.	Salt	To taste
5.	Black cumin powder	¼ tsp
6.	Coriander powder	¼ tsp

METHOD

(1) Heat water in a pan. Put cumin and coriander powder in it. Heat it for 2-3 minutes till it starts giving the flavour.

(2) Add onions and mushroom to the mixture. Cook on low flame for 10 minutes, sprinkle salt on them.

(3) Now put masala on top and again cook for 10-12 minutes.

(4) Serve hot either with rice or chapati.

SOYA ONION

INGREDIENTS

1. Soya beans (soaked in water) — 50 g
2. Onion (small sized) — 5-6
3. Curd — ¼ cup
4. Green chillies — 1-2
5. Salt — To taste
6. Gramflour — 1 tsp
7. Tamarind pulp — 2 tsp
8. Black salt — To taste

METHOD

(1) Heat curd in a pan and add gramflour to it. Heat it on low flame. Put salt and keep on stirring constantly till the mixture becomes thick.

(2) Add sauce and green chillies to it and cook till the chillies have become tender.

(3) Now add soya beans and onion to the mixture. Put water till it becomes thick.

(4) Once the gravy is thick add tamarind pulp.

(5) Serve hot.

ONION WITH CAPSICUM

INGREDIENTS

1. Onions (chopped longitudinally) — 2-3
2. Capsicum (cut oblong) — 2
3. Milk — ½ cup
4. Salt — To taste
5. Turmeric — Pinch
6. Garam Masala — ¼ tsp

METHOD

(1) Heat milk in a pan and add chopped capsicum. Heat it for 10 minutes.

(2) Add salt, turmeric and garam masala to it.

(3) When the capsicum has become tender, add onions.

(4) Sauté both and heat them for 10 minutes.

(5) Serve hot.

Note: Garam Masala: corinander seeds, cumin seeds, black pepper corns, black cumin seeds, dry ginger powder, cardamom, cloves, cinnamon.

TOMATOES

This is one of the most commonly used vegetables. It is also used as a vegetable as such or in a combination. It is of two types.

A. Mumbai origin which is dark red in colour with thick skin and more pulp.
B. Desi, which are native and are grown locally. They are more juicy and with a thin skin. They are sour to taste and are used for jellies, Dips and for preserved preparations.

Let us have a look at some preparations of tomatoes.

STUFFED TOMATOES

INGREDIENTS

1.	Hard tomatoes (Mumbai variety)	4-5
2.	Cottage cheese	¼ cup
3.	Peas (shelled, boiled)	30-40 g
4.	Curd	200 g
5.	Salt	To taste
6.	Black pepper	¼ tsp
7.	Chat masala	¼ tsp

METHOD

(1) Wash the tomatoes and remove the cap. Scoop the pulp from the tomatoes.
(2) Now mix the peas and cheese together. Add black pepper and chat masala to it.
(3) Fill the tomatoes with cheese/peas mixture.
(4) Heat water in a pan. Add the pulp of tomatoes and salt. Heat it for 10 minutes till it becomes thick.
(5) Churn curd thoroughly and mix it with the tomato mixture.
(6) Now cover the lid of tomatoes with the help of a toothpick.
(7) Cook it for 10-15 minutes.
(8) Serve hot.

TOMATO CURRY

INGREDIENTS

1. Tomato pulp — 2-3 tomatoes
2. Vegetables (chopped) Peas (shelled), onion, cauliflower — ¼ cup each
3. Gramflour — 2 tsp
4. Salt — To taste
5. Garam masala — To taste
6. Turmeric powder — To taste

METHOD

(1) Wash tomatoes and make a pulp in the mixer.
(2) Steam all the vegetables and add garam masala to them. Keep them in the chiller for 10-15 minutes.
(3) Heat water in a pan and add tomato pulp to it, cooking on a low flame.
(4) Heat water in other pan and put gramflour in it. Heat it on low flame for 10-12 minutes. Simmer it slowly and now add all the vegetables. Sprinkle turmeric powder and salt over it. Cook it on low flame for 10-15 minutes.
(5) When the tomato pulp becomes thick, add these vegetables to it and cook it for 4-5 minutes.
(6) Serve hot.

Note: Garam Masala: corinander seeds, cumin seeds, black pepper corns, black cumin seeds, dry ginger powder, cardamom, cloves, cinnamon.

TOMATO CHEESE

INGREDIENTS

1.	Tomatoes (medium size)	4-5
2.	Cottage cheese	50 gm
3.	Green chillies (chopped)	1-2
4.	Coriander leaves	A few
5.	Salt and black pepper	To taste
6.	Soya sauce	¼ tsp

METHOD

(1) Put water in a pan and add soya sauce to it. Cook it to for 2-3 minutes.

(2) Cut cheese into small cubes and put it in the soya sauce.

(3) Scoop out the tomato and remove the pulp. Fill the tomato with coriander and chopped chillies, salt and pepper.

(4) When the cheese, sauce mixture has become a little dark, add tomatoes and heat them on low flame or cook them in the oven at 150°F for 10 minutes.

(5) Serve hot either as a vegetable or as a snack with pickle or sauce.

CAULIFLOWER

It is a vegetable grown in northern India. It is a big flower with stem and multiple florets. It is a good source of roughage and Vitamin B6. It is used as a good combination with many vegetables. It has a tendency to have large worms; therefore, it should be washed thoroughly before use.

Let us have a look on different recipes prepared by using cauliflower.

CAULIFLOWER MASALA

INGREDIENTS

1. Masala — ½ cup
2. Cauliflower (big florets) — 8-10
3. Salt — To taste
4. Black pepper — To taste
5. Tamarind pulp — 5-6 tsp
6. Turmeric powder — ¼ tsp
7. Curd — ½ cup
8. Coriander powder — ¼ tsp

METHOD

(1) Heat water in a pan. Put masala into it and cook it on low flame. Now add curd, salt and black pepper. Again cook it for 10-15 minutes.
(2) Steam the cauliflower and put the florets to this mixture. Heat it on low flame. Add turmeric, coriander powder and spread the tamarind pulp and cook it till it is done.
(3) Serve it hot.

CAULIFLOWER WITH POTATOES

INGREDIENTS

1. Steamed Cauliflower — 200 gm
2. Potatoes (medium sized, boiled, cut into pieces) — 2-3
3. Ginger slices — 2-3
4. Green chillies (Cut oblong) — 2
5. Salt — To taste
6. Coriander powder — ¼ tsp
7. Cumin powder — ¼ tsp

METHOD

(1) Heat water in a pan. Put green chillies and ginger in it. Cook it for 5-8 minutes.

(2) Now add coriander powder, cumin and salt.

(3) Mix potatoes and cauliflower, cook on low flame for 15-20 minutes. Serve hot.

CAULIFLOWER WITH PEAS

INGREDIENTS

1. Cauliflower (steamed) — 200 gm
2. Peas (shelled, boiled) — 100 g
3. Ginger slices — 2-3
4. Green chillies (oblong) — 2
5. Salt — To taste
6. Cumin powder and Coriander powder — ¼ tsp
7. Coriander leaves — a few

METHOD

1. Heat water in a pan. Put green chillies and ginger in it. Cook them for 5-8 minutes.
2. Now add coriander powder, cumin and salt.
3. Mix cauliflower and peas, cook them on low flame for 15-20 minutes.
4. Garnish with coriander leaves and serve hot.

CAULIFLOWER KORMA

INGREDIENTS

1.	Cauliflower (steamed)	100 gm
2.	Peas (boiled)	½ cup
3.	Potatoes (small sized, boiled, mashed)	2
4.	Tomato pulp	1 tsp
5.	Curd	½ cup
6.	Salt	To taste
7.	Cumin powder	¼ tsp
8.	Phool makhane	10-12
9.	Coriander powder	¼ tsp

METHOD

(1) Heat water in a pan. Add tomato pulp, salt and phool makhane.

(2) Put the curd in the mixture and cook it for 15-20 minutes. Now add peas, cauliflower and potatoes to it. Mash them thoroughly with a spoon.

(3) Add salt and cook it on low flame for 10-12 minutes.

(4) Serve hot.

PEAS

Peas are a member of the pulse or legume family. It is native to Europe and has been cultivated for over two thousand years. The seed is usually eaten, but there are varieties with edible pods. Green peas may be cooked by steaming for 10-15 minutes. Dried peas must be cooked for longer periods as most are dried beans. It is a good source of carbohydrates and Vitamin E. Let us have a look on different recipe preparations of peas.

PEAS POTATO

INGREDIENTS

1. Peas (boiled) — ½ cup
2. Potatoes (medium sized, boiled) — 2
3. Masala — ¼ cup
4. Salt — To taste
5. Turmeric powder — ¼ tsp
6. Cumin powder — ¼ tsp

METHOD

(1) Heat water in a pan. Add masala and cook it on low flame. Add salt, turmeric powder and cumin powder.
(2) Mix peas in the mixture and cook for 5-10 minutes till they have become soft.
(3) Now add potatoes and water to make the gravy thick.
(4) Cook on low flame and serve hot when it has become thick.

PEAS WITH PANEER

INGREDIENTS

1.	Peas (boiled)	½ cup
2.	Cheese cubes	100 g
3.	Masala	¼ cup
4.	Salt	To taste
5.	Cumin powder	¼ tsp
6.	Chat masala	¼ tsp
7.	Turmeric powder	¼ tsp

METHOD

(1) Heat water in a pan. Add masala and cook it on low flame. Add salt, turmeric powder and cumin powder.

(2) Mix peas and cook for 5-10 minutes till they become soft.

(3) Now add cheese cubes and water to make a thick gravy.

(4) Cook on low flame and sprinkle chat masala.

(5) Serve hot.

PEAS WITH CAULIFLOWER

INGREDIENTS

1. Peas (boiled) — ½ cup
2. Cauliflower (boiled or steamed) — 100 gm
3. Masala — ¼ cup
4. Salt — To taste
5. Cumin powder — To taste
6. Turmeric and coriander powder — ¼ tsp
7. Coriander leaves — A few

METHOD

(1) Heat water in a pan. Add masala and cook on low flame. Add salt, turmeric powder and cumin powder.

(2) Mix cauliflower and peas and cook for 5-10 minutes till they have become soft.

(3) Cook on low flame.

(4) Garnish with coriander leaves and serve hot.

PEAS WITH MUSHROOM

INGREDIENTS

1.	Peas (boiled)	½ cup
2.	Mushroom	100 gm
3.	Masala	¼ cup
4.	Salt	To taste
5.	Cumin powder	To taste
6.	Turmeric and coriander powder	¼ tsp
7.	Coriander leaves	A few
8.	Chat Masala	¼ tsp

METHOD

(1) Heat water in a pan. Add masala and cook it on low flame. Add salt, turmeric powder and cumin powder.

(2) Mix peas and cook for 5-10 minutes till they become soft.

(3) Now add mushroom and water to make a thick gravy.

(4) Cook on low flame.

(5) Garnish with coriander leaves and serve hot when it has become thick.

CARROTS

Carrots which have been cultivated for more than two thousand years in Western Asia were originally white and differed in flavour from the yellow carrots which are popular today. The young carrots are more tender and palpable than the older ones. They become woody as they mature. Carrots are rich in alkaline elements, especially calcium and must have an important place in our diet.

Carrots are rich in carotene. Therefore, carrots help in improving pigmentation and complexion. They are commonly cooked but deserve a wider use in their raw state. In grated form, they can be consumed by weak stomach also. It is a good food for children during weaning. They are also used in jams, jellies, and jellied salads.

Let us have a look on the indigenous combinations of carrots for recipe preparation.

CARROT WITH PEAS

INGREDIENTS

1. Carrots (finely chopped) — 5-6
2. Peas (Boiled) — ½ cup
3. Masala — ¼ cup
4. Salt, cumin powder — To taste
5. Turmeric powder — ¼ tsp
6. Coriander powder — ¼ tsp

METHOD

(1) Heat water in a pan. Add masala and cook on low flame. Add salt, turmeric powder and cumin powder.
(2) Mix peas and carrots and cook for 5-10 minutes till they become soft.
(3) Cook on low flame and serve hot when it becomes thick.

CARROT WITH POTATO

INGREDIENTS

1. Carrots (finely chopped) — 5-6
2. Potatoes (Boiled and cut into pieces) — 2-3
3. Masala — ¼ cup
4. Salt, cumin powder — To taste
5. Turmeric powder — ¼ tsp
6. Coriander powder — ¼ tsp

METHOD

(1) Heat water in a pan. Add masala and cook on low flame. Add salt, turmeric powder and cumin powder.

(2) Mix carrot and cook for 5-10 minutes till they become soft.

(3) Now add potatoes and cook on low flame.

(4) Serve hot.

CARROT WITH PEAS

INGREDIENTS

1.	Carrots (finely chopped)	5-6
2.	Katar (Peeling of pea pods)	50 gm
3.	Masala	¼ cup
4.	Salt, cumin powder	To taste
5.	Turmeric powder	¼ tsp
6.	Coriander powder	¼ tsp

METHOD

(1) Heat water in a pan. Add masala and cook on low flame. Add salt, turmeric powder and cumin powder.

(2) Mix katar and cook for 5-10 minutes till it become soft.

(3) Now add carrot and cook on low flame.

(4) Serve hot.

CABBAGE

This vegetable was at one time considered "vulgar" because of its cheapness. Today, it is highly rated and considered especially valuable for its high mineral and Vitamin content. Cabbage is unique in a manner for the more it is cooked, the more indigestible it becomes. But it is better not to cook it at all, but to eat it raw. In this manner, its minerals and vitamins would not be lost.

It may be cut, fried and boiled, however, for 10 to 15 minutes. It is better served with lemon as compared to vinegar. But recently a microscopic worm has been identified which directly reaches the higher centre (brain) and leads to some neurological symptoms. Therefore, its use has minimized these days.

Let us have a look at some cabbage recipes.

CABBAGE WITH CHEESE

INGREDIENTS

1. Cabbage (small, shredded) — 1
2. Cheese cubes (cut into pieces) — 100 gm
3. Salt — To taste
4. Garlic and ginger slices (oblong) — 2-3
5. Black pepper — To taste

METHOD

(1) Heat water in a pan. Put garlic and ginger slices in it. Heat it for some time.

(2) Add cabbage to it and cook it for 15-20 minutes.

(3) Once it is almost cooked add cheese, salt and black pepper to it.

(4) Serve hot either with pickle or tomato sauce.

CABBAGE WITH PEAS

INGREDIENTS

1. Cabbage (small, finely chopped) — 1
2. Peas (boiled) — 50 gm
3. Salt — To taste
4. Black pepper — To taste
5. Garlic and ginger slices (oblong) — 2-3

METHOD

1. Heat water in a pan. Put garlic and ginger slices. Heat it for some time.

2. Add cabbage and cook it for 15-20 minutes.

3. Once it is almost cooked add boiled peas, salt and black pepper.

4. Serve hot.

CABBAGE WITH MUSHROOMS

INGREDIENTS

1. Cabbage (finely chopped, small sized) — 1
2. Mushroom — 50 gm
3. Salt — To taste
4. Cumin powder — ¼ tsp
5. Soya sauce — 2-3 tsp
6. Garlic and ginger slices (oblong) — 2-3

METHOD

(1) Heat water in a pan. Put garlic and ginger slices. Heat it for some time.

(2) Now add soya sauce and cumin powder. Mix well.

(3) Add cabbage and cook it for 10-15 minutes.

(4) Once it is half cooked, add mushroom, salt and black pepper. Cook on low flame for another 10 minutes.

(5) Serve hot.

BEANS

Under this heading, we may consider all forms of dry seed beans in common use with the exception of Soya bean. The three types most commonly used are lima beans, the navy or white pea beans and the red kidney beans.

The nutritive properties of the varying beans are quite similar with high elements of proteins. The mineral content of all beans is strongly alkaline. The lima beans are freshly shelled from the pods as peas. They are more palatable as well as get quickly cooked when they are dry. The cooking process is enhanced by prior soaking the beans overnight.

The string beans which are usually eaten as a tender pod are quite different from the native bean seeds. They are as unpalatable raw as any other vegetable. They should be either steamed or cooked on low flame.

Soya bean was originally grown in Japan and China. It is rich in fats and proteins. It has got the highest protein content amongst the vegetable foods. It is also used as flour for diabetic breads. It is also used to make Soya milk and Soya cheese. Soya bean oil is also used extensively for cooking.

BEANS WITH POTATO

It is the commonest combination. It is prepared on low flame.

INGREDIENTS

1.	Beans (cut finely)	100 gm
2.	Potatoes (small sized, cut finely)	2
3.	Masala	¼ cup
4.	Salt	To taste
5.	Chat masala	To taste
6.	Coriander powder	¼ tsp

METHOD

1. Heat water in a saucepan. Put the masala (paste) and heat it on low flame. Cook it thoroughly till it starts giving the flavour.
2. Add salt, coriander powder and potatoes. Allow it to cook for some time.
3. When potatoes are soft, put green beans. Heat on low flame.
4. When tender, sprinkle chat masala and serve hot.

PUMPKIN

The pumpkin, squash and "vegetable marrow" are members of the gourd family. There are two types of squash: summer and winter. Summer squashes are cooked and eaten without peeling or removing the seeds. But the thick rimed winter squash is inedible. This squash is best baked, as is the pumpkin. It is rich in vitamin A and minerals.

Let us have a look on some of its recipes:

INGREDIENTS

1. Pumpkin (small, cut into small pieces) — 1
2. Masala — ¼ cup
3. Salt, black pepper, cumin powder — To taste
4. Turmeric powder — ¼ tsp

METHOD

(1) Heat water in a pan. Add masala and cook it for 15-20 minutes.

(2) Put the cut slices of pumpkin. Sprinkle salt, turmeric, black pepper and cumin.

(3) Cover it and cook it on low flame. After 10-15 minutes, it is ready to be served.

SWEET PUMPKIN

It also belongs to the gourd family. It is rich in Vitamin A and Vitamin K. It is a large fruit and is used both as a vegetable and a sweet. Let us have a look on its preparation.

INGREDIENTS

1. Sweet pumpkin (Petha) (sliced) — 200 gm
2. Onion and green chillies (chopped) — 1 each
3. Ginger (chopped) — 5-6 slices
4. Salt — To taste
5. Sugar — 10-20 gm
6. Mango powder — ¼ tsp
7. Black salt — To taste
8. Cumin powder — ¼ tsp

METHOD

(1) Heat water in a pan.
(2) Put chopped onions, ginger and chillies in it.
(3) Heat them on low flame. Now add the chopped slices of sweet pumpkin.
(4) Add salt, sugar, black salt, cumin powder and mango powder to the vegetables.
(5) Mix them thoroughly. Serve hot.

BITTER GOURD

It is a good vegetable rich in vitamin A, vitamin C and minerals. It is long, greenish in colour with a strong aromatic odour and is bitter to taste.

STUFFED BITTER GOURD

INGREDIENTS

1.	Bitter Gourd (Karela) (medium sized)	5-6
2.	Onions (chopped)	2-3
3.	Salt	To taste
4.	Black pepper	To taste
5.	Turmeric powder	¼ tsp
6.	Tamarind pulp	2 tsp

METHOD

(1) Wash the bitter gourds thoroughly. Then, make a cut in their middle.
(2) Chop onions and heat them in a pan. Add salt, turmeric powder and cumin to the onions. Cook them till the mixture becomes dry.
(3) Now fill the bitter gourd with this mixture and then close them with a toothpick, so that the filling will not spill out.
(4) Heat water in a deep pan, and allow it to boil. When it has become a bit thick, add tamarind pulp and bitter gourds into it. Cover the lid. Cook on low flame for a few minutes.
(5) Serve hot.

CHOPPED BITTER GOURD

INGREDIENTS

1.	Bitter Gourd (chopped)	2-3
2.	Potatoes (small, chopped)	2
3.	Green chillies	2-3
4.	Onions (finely chopped, medium size)	2 s
5.	Salt	¼ tsp
6.	Turmeric powder	¼ tsp
7.	Garam masala	To taste

METHOD

(1) Sprinkle salt on the karelas and chopped onions.

(2) Keep them so for 3-4 hours, so that the extra water is drained out.

(3) Heat water in a pan and cook potatoes, add karelas and then last of all the onions. When they are cooked add garam masala and turmeric powder .

(4) Serve hot.

Note: Garam Masala: corinander seeds, cumin seeds, black pepper corns, black cumin seeds, dry ginger powder, cardamom, cloves, cinnamon.

LADY FINGER

It is a so called green vegetable but it does not have any value of the greens. It just gives starch and roughage.

Let us have a look at some preparations of Lady finger:

STUFFED LADY FINGER

INGREDIENTS

1. Lady finger — 200 gm
2. Onion & garlic (chopped, medium sized) — 1
3. Fresh paneer — 100 gm
4. Salt — To taste
5. Mango powder — ¼ tsp

METHOD

(1) Wash the lady finger. Dry them and make a cut in the centre.
(2) Heat them in the microwave for 2-3 minutes so that the stickiness is reduced to the minimum.
(3) Now heat water in a pan, add cheese and chopped onions, and garlic. Make a mixture, till it becomes thick. Put salt and mango powder.
(4) Fill this mixture into the lady finger and close them so that spilling is avoided.
(5) Heat them in the microwave for 10 minutes at 950 watt or heat them in a minimum quantity of water in a pan, uncovered so that the sticky discharge it released.
(6) Serve with curd.

CHOPPED LADY FINGER

INGREDIENTS

1.	Lady fingers (chopped)	200 gm
2.	Onions (chopped, small)	2
3.	Potatoes (chopped, small)	1
4.	Salt	To taste
5.	Curd	2-3 tsp

METHOD

(1) Heat pan and add curd. To this add, potatoes and onions. Put garam masala and cook them till they have become soft.

(2) Chop the lady fingers and add to the pan. When half cooked put salt in it. Cook it on low flame, slightly uncovered.

(3) When tender, serve hot.

Note: Garam Masala: corinander seeds, cumin seeds, black pepper corns, black cumin seeds, dry ginger powder, cardamom, cloves, cinnamon.

EGGPLANT

They are a good source of vitamin A and roughage. Otherwise they have a limited nutritional value of their own. They are available in two sizes, round ones, and the small ones also known as chuchu.

EGGPLANT BHARTHA

INGREDIENTS

1.	Eggplant (Round, medium)	1
2.	Onions (chopped)	4-5
3.	Tomatoes (chopped)	2-3
4.	Green chillies (chopped)	2
5.	Salt	To taste
6.	Garam masala	½ tsp
7.	Coriander powder	To taste

METHOD

(1) Wash the Eggplant and cut it into pieces. Boil it in the pressure cooker. When it has become cool, peel off the skin and mash the boiled eggplant.

(2) Heat water in a pan and cook onion on low flame. When slightly pinkish add tomatoes and green chillies.

(3) Cook them on low flame and add salt and garam masala. When the mixture has become thick, keep on stirring in between so that it is mashed and cooked properly.

(4) Now add the mashed Eggplant. Again cook on low flame till it is mixed up thoroughly. Sprinkle Coriander powder and serve hot.

(5) The Eggplant mixture can be added to curd and can serve as a nutritious raita also.

Note: Garam Masala: corinander seeds, cumin seeds, black pepper corns, black cumin seeds, dry ginger powder, cardamom, cloves, cinnamon.

POTATO WITH EGGPLANT

INGREDIENTS

1. Potatoes (cut into pieces) — 2-3
2. Eggplants (small ones) — 5 to 6
3. Masala — ¼ cup
4. Salt — To taste
5. Turmeric powder — ¼ tsp
6. Mango powder — ¼ tsp

METHOD

(1) Heat water in a pan, add masala to it and cook it on low flame.

(2) Mix salt and mango powder and keep them aside.

(3) Wash the eggplants and give a cut in the middle. Fill the mixture of salt and mango powder in them.

(4) When masala has thickened cook these eggplants on low flame. When half cooked, add potatoes and turmeric powder.

(5) Put water and cook on low flame till they are cooked thoroughly.

(6) Serve with bread or chapati.

COLOCASIA WITH EGGPLANT

INGREDIENTS

1. Colocasia (arvi) (cut into long pieces) — 4-5
2. Eggplant (small) — 4-5
3. Masala — ¼ cup
4. Salt — To taste
5. Mango powder — To taste
6. Turmeric powder — To taste

METHOD

1. Heat water in a pan, add masala to it and cook it on low flame.
2. Mix salt and mango powder and keep them aside.
3. Wash the eggplants and give a cut in the middle. Fill the mixture of salt and mango powder in the cut.
4. When masala gets thickened, put these eggplants in a pan and cook on low flame. When half cooked, add colocasia and turmeric powder.
5. Put water and cook on low flame till they are cooked thoroughly.
6. Serve with bread or chapati.

COLOCASIA WITH ONIONS

It is equally a good and widely available vegetable with a rich source of starch and carbohydrates. It has got a thin sticky gluey discharge and has an aromatic odour. Let us have a look on the recipes.

INGREDIENTS

1. Colocasia (chopped into long thin pieces) — 5-6
2. Onion (chopped oblong) — 2-3
3. Green chillies (chopped) — 2
4. Salt, cumin, turmeric powder — To taste

METHOD

(1) Heat water in a pan. Add green chillies and onion to it. Heat for 10-12 minutes.

(2) Peel, wash and cut colocasia into pieces. Add this to the onion. When half cooked sprinkle salt, cumin and turmeric powder. When cooked thoroughly, serve hot.

EGGPLANT WITH COLOCASIA

INGREDIENTS

1.	Colocasia (arvi) cut into long pieces	4-5
2.	Eggplant (small)	4-5
3.	Masala	¼ cup
4.	Salt	To taste
5.	Mango powder	To taste
6.	Turmeric powder	To taste

METHOD

(1) Heat water in a pan, add masala to it and cook it on low flame.

(2) Mix salt and mango powder and keep them aside.

(3) Wash the eggplants and give a cut in the middle. Fill the mixture of salt and mango powder in the cut.

(4) When masala gets thickened cook these eggplants on low flame. When half cooked, add colocasia and turmeric powder.

(5) Put water and cook on low flame till they are cooked thoroughly.

(6) Serve with bread or chapati.

MASALA COLOCASIA

INGREDIENTS

1.	Arvi (boiled and peeled)	10-12 pieces
2.	Green chillies (chopped)	2
3.	Masala	¼ cup
4.	Curd	¼ cup
5.	Salt	To taste
6.	Garam masala	¼ tsp
7.	Mango powder	¼ tsp

METHOD

(1) Boil colocasia and peel the skin gently.

(2) Heat water in a pan and cook masala for 20-25 minutes. When thick, add curd and chopped green chillies, mango powder, salt and garam masala.

(3) Now put the boiled arvi, mix it thoroughly. Put some water to make thick gravy. When cooked, serve hot.

Note: Garam Masala: corinander seeds, cumin seeds, black pepper corns, black cumin seeds, dry ginger powder, cardamom, cloves, cinnamon.

VEGETABLE KARHI

INGREDIENTS

CHOPPED VEGETABLES

1.	Carrot	2
2.	Peas	50 gm
3.	Onion (chopped)	1
4.	Potatoes (chopped)	2
5.	Curd	1 cup
6.	Gramflour	3-4 tsp
7.	Salt	To taste
8.	Cumin (Black)	¼ tsp
9.	Garam masala	¼ tsp
10.	Turmeric powder	¼ tsp
11.	Curry leaves	2

METHOD

(1) Mix gramflour and curd, churn them in the mixer to make a thick batter.
(2) Heat water in a pan, sprinkle cumin seeds and curry leaves.
(3) Add all chopped vegetables. Cook them for 10-15 minutes. Put salt, garam masala and turmeric powder into it.
(4) When fully cooked add gramflour/curd batter, cover it and cook on low flame. Allow it to boil, when it becomes thick, serve hot.

Note: Garam Masala: corinander seeds, cumin seeds, black pepper corns, black cumin seeds, dry ginger powder, cardamom, cloves, cinnamon.

CAPSICUM

It is native to the capsicum Anne family. It is available in different colours namely green, orange, yellow and red. It has an aromatic odour and is rich in minerals. It has a good roughage value.

Let us have a look on its different recipes.

STUFFED CAPSICUM

INGREDIENTS

1. Capsicum (medium size) — 5-6
2. Potatoes (boiled, mashed) — 2
3. Curd — ¼ cup
4. Salt — To taste
5. Garam masala and cumin powder — ¼ tsp each

METHOD

(1) Wash the capsicum and scoop them out. Remove the seeds and keep the caps separately.
(2) Mash the potatoes. Add salt, cumin powder and garam masala. Mix it well.
(3) Fill this mixture into the empty capsicums and cover up the caps with the help of tooth pick or match stick.
(4) Heat water in a pan. Put curd and add salt. Allow it to become thick. Put the capsicums in the pan and heat them on low flame till they turn light yellow.
(5) Serve hot.

Note: Garam Masala: corinander seeds, cumin seeds, black pepper corns, black cumin seeds, dry ginger powder, cardamom, cloves, cinnamon.

CAPSICUM WITH POTATO

INGREDIENTS

1.	Capsicum (cut into pieces)	5-6
2.	Potatoes (boiled, cut into pieces)	4-5
3.	Masala	¼ cup
4.	Salt	To taste
5.	Cumin powder	To taste
6.	Turmeric powder	¼ tsp
7.	Garlic flakes	2-3

METHOD

(1) Heat water in a pan. Add garlic flakes and heat them on low flame till it leaves its flavour. Add masala and heat it for 15-20 minutes.

(2) Now put potatoes and capsicum into the mixture. Cook on low flame for 20-25 minutes. When it starts steaming, add turmeric powder, salt and cumin powder.

(3) Serve hot.

CAPSICUM PANEER

INGREDIENTS

1. Capsicum (medium sized, cut into pieces)   2-3
2. Paneer cubes   100
3. Masala   ½ cup
4. Salt   To taste
5. Cumin powder   ¼ tsp
6. Turmeric powder   ¼ tsp

METHOD

1. Heat water in a pan. Add masala and heat for 15-20 minutes.
2. Now put capsicum. Cook on low flame for 10-15 minutes. When it starts steaming add turmeric powder, salt and cumin powder.
3. Now add paneer cubes and cook on low flame for 5 minutes.
4. Serve hot.

RADISH

It is a highly beneficial vegetable with leaves which has a strong medicinal value. The root as a whole is a good source of calcium, vitamin A. Its leaves are a source of vitamin C and minerals. The cap of radish is the richest source of calcium.

Let us have a look on some of its recipe preparations.

GRATED RADISH

INGREDIENTS

1.	Radish (small, grated)	1
2.	Ginger (grated)	50 g
3.	Green chillies (chopped)	2-3
4.	Salt	To taste
5.	Black Pepper	To taste
6.	Mustard seeds	Few

METHOD

(1) Heat water in a pan. Put mustard seeds in it. When they start sparkling, add ginger and grated radish.

(2) Cook on low flame, add green chillies, salt and black pepper.

(3) Cook them until they become dry.

(4) Serve hot with bajra Indian bread or Cornflour bread.

RADISH WITH POTATO

INGREDIENTS

1.	Radish (small, cut into pieces)	1
2.	Potato (cut into pieces)	2-3
3.	Masala	¼ cup
4.	Salt	To taste
5.	Cumin powder	¼ tsp
6.	Turmeric	¼ tsp

METHOD

(1) Heat water in a pan. Add masala and cook it for 10-15 minutes.

(2) Once it is cooked, add radish and potato with little water and keep it on low flame. Once it is half cooked, put salt in it.

(3) When the gravy gets thick, serve hot.

NUTTY MUTTY GINGER

A wonderful nut remedy wherein crushed almonds and walnuts are used. It is a wonderful ANTIOXIDANT also.

INGREDIENTS

1.	Almonds (soaked)	6-8
2.	Ginger (cut pieces)	20 gm
3.	Garlic (cut pieces)	20 gm
4.	Salt	To Taste
5.	Red chilly flakes	Few

METHOD

1. Take 3 cups of water. Let the waters boil for 5-7 minutes. Once boiled add cut flakes of ginger, garlic and almonds. Boil the mixture for at least 10 mins and allow it to cool. Once cool, add chilly flakes and salt.
2. Serve hot with garlic bread or roasted bread slice.

FLOATING SPRING ONIONS

INGREDIENTS

1.	Spring onions	10-15 sticks
2.	Tomatoes (grated)	3-4
3.	Fenugreek leaves	¼ tsp
4.	Cardamom	2
5.	Garam masala	Pinch
6.	Black salt	Pinch

METHOD

(1) Take 15-20 twigs of fresh spring onions. Soak them in water for 15-20 minutes so that their acidic taste goes away.

(2) Heat water in a pan, add tomato puree and cover it for 10 minutes. Once it starts boiling add fenugreek leaves & cardamom.

(3) Again keep it covered on low flame, once it becomes thick add water to make it more watery.

(4) Keep it on low flame and add spring onions with a cut in between the sticks.

(5) Switch off the flame. Cook them in steam for 5 minutes.

(6) Serve hot with naan or Indian bread.

Note: Garam Masala: corinander seeds, cumin seeds, black pepper corns, black cumin seeds, dry ginger powder, cardamom, cloves, cinnamon.

SWEET 'N' SOUR JUGNU

INGREDIENTS

1.	Jugnu (Petha long)	1 piece
2.	Brown sugar	2-3 tsp
3.	Mango powder	¼ tsp
4.	Linseed	½ tsp
5.	Cloves	2
6.	Salt	¼ tsp

METHOD

(1) Wash jugnu and cut it into small pieces.

(2) Put 2-3 tsp of water in a pan, add cloves and linseed. Allow them to splitter.

(3) Add cut pieces of jugnu and steam on low flame. Once they become soft, add sugar and salt.

(4) Keep it covered for another 5-7 minutes. Switch off the flame.

(5) Once it is through, add mango powder and serve hot with naan or Indian bread.

HEENG-E-MATAR

INGREDIENTS

1.	Green fresh peas or dry matar (Boiled)	200 gm
2.	Asafetida (Heeng)	10 gm
3.	Cumin powder	1 tsp
4.	Lemon juice/tamarind juice	3 tsp
5.	Garam masala	Pinch
6.	Black salt	¼ tsp
7.	Onion chopped	2 small

METHOD

(1) Take a steamer and steam peas for 10-15 minutes if they are fresh. If they are dry, boil them or pressure cook for 20 minutes till they become soft.

(2) Soak peas in ½ litre water with cumin, asafetida, garam masala and black salt.

(3) Put them on low flame till they become little softer.

(4) Put off the flame and add chopped onions and lemon/tamarind juice.

(5) Serve them with either garlic bread or hot buns.

Note: Garam Masala: corinander seeds, cumin seeds, black pepper corns, black cumin seeds, dry ginger powder, cardamom, cloves, cinnamon.

MALAI KOFTA

INGREDIENTS

1.	Gramflour or flour	100 gm
2.	Potatoes or Paneer (grated)	100 gm
3.	Tomato puree	250 gm
4.	Fenugreek leaves	Pinch
5.	Garam masala	Pinch
6.	Vegetable masala dry	2 tsp

METHOD

(1) Mix gramflour or flour with paneer or potatoes. Make soft balls and put them in a nonstick pan to turn them golden brown.

(2) Keep a small pan and put tomato puree with Fenugreek leaves in it.

(3) Allow it to be steamed on low flame. Once it gets boiled, put dry masala and little bit of water to make more gravy.

(4) Once the gravy is thick, remove it from the flame and add garam masala and the kofta balls.

(5) Before serving put cream. Serve hot with Indian bread or naan.

Note: Garam Masala: corinander seeds, cumin seeds, black pepper corns, black cumin seeds, dry ginger powder, cardamom, cloves, cinnamon.

BEETROOT

It is a tuber and rich in carotene and vitamin A. it is also used as a colouring agent for various preservatives. It is rich in vitamin A and along with carrots is used for juices of vegetable origin.

INGREDIENTS

1. Potatoes (boiled) — 4-5 medium size
2. Beetroot (boiled) — 1
3. Curd — 50 gm
4. Fenugreek leaves — ¼ tsp
5. Black salt — ¼ tsp
6. Cumin powder — Pinch

METHOD

(1) Put curd in a small pan and add fenugreek leaves.

(2) Let it boil for 2-3 minutes.

(3) Add cut, boiled potatoes and salt with cumin powder.

(4) Mix them thoroughly. Once it is cool, add beetroot.

(5) Serve with Indian bread or bread.

NUTTY MUTTY RADISH

INGREDIENTS

1. Walnuts (Soaked) — 100 gm
2. radish (Grated) — 250 gm
3. Salt — ¼ tsp
4. Tamarind — Pinch

METHOD

(1) Take a small pan. Heat 2-3 tsp of water.

(2) Put grated radish and steam it on low flame for 10-15 minutes.

(3) Once it is cooked, add turmeric, salt and before you take it off flame add walnuts.

(4) Serve with Cornflour bread.

LOTUS STEM WITH CHEESE

INGREDIENTS

1.	Lotus stem (Kamal kakdi) (Cut into small pieces)	250 gm
2.	Cheese slices	2
3.	Curd	100 gm
4.	Black salt	¼ tsp
5.	Garam masala	Pinch
6.	Red chilly flakes	¼ tsp

METHOD

(1) Steam the lotus steam to make it soft and tender.

(2) Put curd in a pan, allow it to heat for few minutes.

(3) Once it is hot, add salt, garam masala and cheese slices.

(4) Once it becomes thick add pieces of lotus stem and cook it on low flame for 10 minutes.

(5) Serve hot with Indian bread or naan.

NOTE: *To make it more delicious, sprinkle either mango powder or few drops of lemon.*

PANEER AND ITS PREPARATION

PANEER

- Paneer Korma
- Shahi Paneer
- Paneer ki Bhurji
- Paneer ka Tikka
- Paneer Sizzler
- Paneer Chiller
- Paneer with Peas
- Paneer with Cauliflower
- Paneer with Chickpeas
- Paneer with Lobhia
- Roxy/boxy Paneer
- Paneer with Colocasia
- Nutty Ginger Paneer
- Shahi Korma

MODE OF PREPARATION:

1. Take 250 ml skimmed milk. Allow it to boil. When on the verge of boiling add 2-3 teaspoons of lemon juice. Again allow it to heat on low flame with a covered lid. When the

milk protein and liquid starts getting separated add a pinch of salt.

2. After 5-6 minutes, the milk protein gets separated. Take a muslin cloth and strain the product. Hang the cheese portion and put some weight over it so that the extra water is drained out.
3. When it is set, cut it into pieces and use it for cooking.
4. Paneer ka pani is good for nourishment and can be used as a drink for obesity, for diabetes and in I.B.S. (irritable bowel syndrome)

Flavours: It can be made in different flavours and colours by adding different Ingredients. Let us have a look.

Tomato/Red Paneer: When the separation of milk takes place, add tomato pulp 2-3 teaspoons.

Green/Minty Paneer: Add mint leaves for flavour. To add green colour, mix grated mint leaves or coriander leaves.

Soya Paneer: To the preparation, add Soya granules or powdered Soya.

Yellow Paneer: To this add turmeric or yellow colour with few leaves of saffron.

Let us have a look on different paneer recipes.

PANEER KORMA

INGREDIENTS

1.	Paneer (mashed)	½ cup
2.	Onions (small, chopped)	1
3.	Tomatoes (chopped)	1
4.	Green chillies (chopped)	2
5.	Salt	To taste
6.	Chat masala	¼ tsp
7.	Phool makhane or roasted sabudana	¼ cup
8.	Pulsechini	2 twigs
9.	Cloves	2-3
10.	Khoya (grated)	50 gm
11.	Cumin powder	¼ tsp

METHOD

(1) Heat water in a pan. Add pulsechini, cloves and green chillies. Allow it to heat for 5-6 minutes till it leaves its flavour.

(2) Add chopped onions, phool makhane/sabudana and allow it to cook for 10-12 minutes on low flame. Add salt, cumin and chat masala.

(3) Now add tomatoes and khoya together so that there is no need to add water.

(4) Allow it to cook for 20-25 minutes, when mixture becomes thick, add grated paneer. Mix all thoroughly and cook it on low flame for 5-6 minutes.

(5) Garnish with coriander leaves.

SHAHI PANEER

INGREDIENTS

1. Tomatoes (big, chopped, blended) — 5-6
2. Ginger slices 1" — 5-6
3. Green chillies (cut oblong) — 4-5
4. Milk (toned) — ½ cup
5. Paneer cubes — 150 gm
6. Small cardamom — 2
7. Salt — To taste
8. Chat masala — ¼ tsp
9. Garam masala — ¼ tsp

METHOD

(1) Heat water in a pan; add small cardamom and garam masala in it. Add ginger slices and tomato pulp. Cook it for 15-20 minutes till it becomes thick.

(2) To make a good gravy, add milk and again heat it for 10-15 minutes.

(3) When gravy has become thick, add paneer cubes and mix them thoroughly.

(4) Serve hot, garnished with coriander/mint leaves.

Note: Garam Masala: corinander seeds, cumin seeds, black pepper corns, black cumin seeds, dry ginger powder, cardamom, cloves, cinnamon.

HARYALI PANEER

INGREDIENTS

1.	Coriander leaves (chopped, grated)	¼ cup
2.	Curd (beaten)	¼ cup
3.	Green chillies (cut oblong)	2-3
4.	Mint leaves (chopped)	Few
5.	Radish leaves	Few
6.	Paneer cubes	1 cup
7.	Salt	To taste
8.	Chat masala	¼ tsp

METHOD

(1) Heat water in a pan. Put garam masala, chopped coriander leaves and beaten curd in it and cook it on a low flame. Now add water and make the mixture thick for gravy.

(2) When it becomes thick add green chillies, chat masala and salt.

(3) Again cook it for 10-12 minutes. Mix the paneer cubes thoroughly.

(4) If mixture is quite thick, add some water or milk. Garnish with mint and radish leaves.

(5) Serve hot.

Note: Garam Masala: corinander seeds, cumin seeds, black pepper corns, black cumin seeds, dry ginger powder, cardamom, cloves, cinnamon.

SCRAMBLED PANEER

INGREDIENTS

1.	Paneer (mashed)	1 cup
2.	Onions (chopped, medium)	1
3.	Tomatoes (chopped, small)	1
4.	Green chillies (small)	2
5.	Salt	To taste
6.	Turmeric	¼ tsp
7.	Chat masala	¼ tsp

METHOD

(1) Heat water in a pan; put green chillies and onions in it. Heat them on low flame for 10 minutes. Add chat masala to it followed by turmeric powder and tomatoes.

(2) Mix it thoroughly and again heat on low flame. Put salt in it and allow the tomatoes to cook.

(3) When the mixture becomes thick add mashed paneer. Mix it thoroughly and garnish with coriander leaves.

(4) Serve hot.

PANEER TIKKA

INGREDIENTS

1.	Paneer cubes	10-15
2.	Gramflour solution (thin)	¼ cup
3.	Salt	To taste
4.	Cumin powder	¼ tsp
5.	Black salt	¼ tsp
6.	Chat masala and garam masala	¼ tsp
7.	Soda bicarbonate	A pinch

METHOD

(1) Cut paneer into cubical pieces.
(2) Make a thin batter of gramflour and add salt, cumin, black salt, garam masala to it.
(3) Put garam masala and chat masala together in a plate. Roll the paneer.
(4) Pass these cubes one by one on the bar and the extra gramflour to trickle the cubes.
(5) Heat on low flame by holding it with a holder or grill in the over for 10-15 minutes.
(6) Serve hot with tomato sauce.

Note: Garam Masala: corinander seeds, cumin seeds, black pepper corns, black cumin seeds, dry ginger powder, cardamom, cloves, cinnamon.

PANEER SIZZLER

INGREDIENTS

1. Paneer cubes — 10-15
2. Capsicum (small, cut long) — 2-3
3. Onions (medium sized, cut long) — 2-3
4. Beans (cut long) — 10-15
5. Salt — To taste
6. Garam masala — ¼ tsp
7. Chat masala — ¼ tsp

METHOD

(1) Heat water in a pan and add onions and cook them for 5-10 minutes.

(2) Once it is cooked; put beans and capsicum. Allow them to heat on low flame. Add chat masala, salt and again cover it on low flame.

(3) When the vegetables are cooked, mix paneer cubes and heat it on low flame only for 2 minutes.

(4) Spread garam masala and serve steaming hot.

Note: Garam Masala: corinander seeds, cumin seeds, black pepper corns, black cumin seeds, dry ginger powder, cardamom, cloves, cinnamon.

PANEER CHILLER

INGREDIENTS

1.	Paneer cubes	10-15
2.	Curd (beaten)	1 cup
3.	Tomato puree	3-4 tsp
4.	Mint leaves	Few twigs
5.	Garam masala	To taste
6.	Salt	To taste
7.	Sugar (powdered)	2-3 tsp

METHOD

(1) Beat curd and mix tomato puree, salt, and garam masala in it.

(2) Heat water in a pan and keep the paneer in it for 10 minutes. Drain the water and dry the paneer.

(3) Keep the curd in the chilller. Once chilled, mix sugar, paneer cubes and garnish them with mint leaves.

(4) Serve chilled.

Note: Garam Masala: coriander seeds, cumin seeds, black pepper corns, black cumin seeds, dry ginger powder, cardamom, cloves, cinnamon.

PANEER WITH PEAS

INGREDIENTS

1. Peas (Boiled) — ½ cup
2. Cheese cubes — 100 g
3. Masala — ¼ cup
4. Salt — To taste
5. Cumin powder — ¼ tsp
6. Turmeric powder — ¼ tsp
7. Chat masala — ¼ tsp

METHOD

(1) Heat water in a pan. Add masala and cook on low flame. Add salt, turmeric powder and cumin powder.

(2) Mix peas and cook for 5-10 minutes till they become soft.

(3) Now add cheese cubes and water to make a thick gravy.

(4) Cook on low flame and sprinkle chat masala.

(5) Serve hot.

PANEER SPINACH

INGREDIENTS

1. Paneer cubes — 100 gm
2. Spinach leaves (washed, chopped) — 250 gm
3. Green chillies (chopped) — 2
4. Salt, black pepper, cumin powder — To Taste
5. Cloves — 2

METHOD

(1) Heat water in a pan, put cloves, cumin powder, green chillies and salt. Heat it for 1-2 minutes.

(2) Wash the spinach. Then, add it to the mixture and steam spinach for 5-7 minutes on covered flame. Allow it to cool, mash slightly with soft hands.

(3) Now add paneer cubes and cook for another 5 minutes.

(4) Serve hot.

PANEER WITH CAULIFLOWER

INGREDIENTS

1. Cauliflower florets — 1 cup
2. Paner cubes — ½ cup
3. Masala (refer to vegetable section) — ¼ cup
4. Salt — To taste
5. Chat masala — ¼ tsp
6. Turmeric powder — ¼ tsp
7. Garam masala — Pinch

METHOD

(1) Steam cauliflower florets for 5-7 minutes.

(2) Heat water in a pan and put garam masala and the masala. Cook it on low flame. When it gets cooked, mix florets, salt, turmeric powder and chat masala. Again cook on low flame.

(3) Now add cubes of paneer to the mixture.

(4) Heat on low flame and garnish with coriander leaves.

(5) Serve hot.

Note: Garam Masala: corinander seeds, cumin seeds, black pepper corns, black cumin seeds, dry ginger powder, cardamom, cloves, cinnamon.

PANEER WITH CHICKPEAS

INGREDIENTS

1.	Paneer cubes	1 cup
2.	Chickpeas	¼ cup
3.	Masala	¼ cup
4.	Salt	To taste
5.	Garam masala	Pinch
6.	Turmeric powder	¼ tsp
7.	Chat masala	¼ tsp

METHOD

(1) Steam Chickpeas for 5-7 minutes.

(2) Heat water in a pan and put garam masala and masala. Cook it on low flame. When it gets cooked, mix chickpeas, salt, turmeric powder, and chat masala. Again cook on low flame.

(3) Now add cubes of paneer.

(4) Heat on low flame and garnish with coriander leaves.

(5) Serve hot.

Note: Garam Masala: corinander seeds, cumin seeds, black pepper corns, black cumin seeds, dry ginger powder, cardamom, cloves, cinnamon.

PANEER WITH LOBHIA

INGREDIENTS

1. Paneer cubes	1 cup
2. Red lobhia (boiled)	½ cup
3. Masala	¼ cup
4. Salt	To taste
5. Chat masala	To taste
6. Coriander leaves	¼ tsp

METHOD

(1) Soak lobhia for 2-3 hrs. Then, boil it in the cooker.

(2) Heat water in a pan and add masala in it. Cook it for sometime. Now add chat masala, garam masala and salt.

(3) Once it gets cooked, add boiled lobhia and cover it and cook on low flame for 10-15 minutes.

(4) Once the gravy is thick, mix cubes of paneer and garnish it with coriander leaves.

(5) Serve hot.

Note: Garam Masala: corinander seeds, cumin seeds, black pepper corns, black cumin seeds, dry ginger powder, cardamom, cloves, cinnamon.

ROXY-BOXY PANEER

INGREDIENTS

1. Single big cube of paneer
2. Pomengranate (peeled) — ½ katori
3. Mint leaves — Few twigs
4. Sugar solution with lemon — 5-6 tsp
5. Tomato pulp — 2-3 tsp
6. Coriander leaves (blended) — Few
7. Salt — To taste
8. Chat masala — To taste

METHOD

(1) Make a scoop in the cube of paneer and take off the cap. Make small holes in the cube with the help of a fork.

(2) Now mix blended coriander and sugar lemon solution. Pour this mixed solution in the paneer box drop by drop.

(3) Mix salt, chat masala and tomato pulp together, fill this mixture into the empty paneer box. Cover it up with the lid.

(4) Grill it in the microwave for 10-12 minutes.

(5) Garnish with mint leaves and pomegranate and serve hot.

PANEER WITH COLOCASIA

INGREDIENTS

1.	Arvi (colocasia) (boiled, peeled)	10-12 pieces
2.	Paneer cubes	½ cup
3.	Masala	¼ cup
4.	Salt	To taste
5.	Garam masala	Pinch
6.	Turmeric powder	¼ tsp
7.	Chat masala	¼ tsp

METHOD

(1) Heat water in a pan. Add masala and cook on low flame.

(2) Mix salt, garam masala and turmeric powder. When the mixture becomes thick, add pieces of cut colocasia. Mix water to make a thick gravy.

(3) Now add paneer cubes. Mix together. Add chat masala and serve hot, garnished with coriander leaves.

Note: Garam Masala: corinander seeds, cumin seeds, black pepper corns, black cumin seeds, dry ginger powder, cardamom, cloves, cinnamon.

NUTTY GINGER PANEER

INGREDIENTS

1.	Paneer cubes	½ cup
2.	Ginger slices ½" oblong	2-3
3.	Chat masala	¼ tsp
4.	Kari patta	¼ tsp
5.	Big cardamom	¼ tsp
6.	Kishmish	10-12
7.	Cashew (soaked)	5-6
8.	Almonds (soaked)	5-6
9.	Curd	5-6 tsp
10.	Salt	To taste
11.	Garam masala	¼ tsp
12.	Coriander leaves (chopped)	Few

METHOD

(1) Heat water in a pan. Put big cardamom, karhi patta and garam masala into it. When it gets heated, add ginger slices and allow it to cook for 10-12 minutes.

(2) When the aroma starts steaming, add green chillies, chat masala and salt.

(3) Blend all the nuts in the blender, mix the curd and make a thick gravy paste.

(4) Mix it in the pan and heat it for 10-15 minutes. When the mixture gets thick, add paneer cubes.

(5) Garnish with coriander leaves and serve hot.

Note: Garam Masala: corinander seeds, cumin seeds, black pepper corns, black cumin seeds, dry ginger powder, cardamom, cloves, cinnamon.

SHAHI KORMA

INGREDIENTS

1. Tomato puree/paste of tomatoes — 4 tsp
2. Fenugreek leaves — ½ tsp
3. Cottage cheese — 100 gm
4. Fresh peas — 100 gm
5. Phool makhana — 100 gm (soaked in water)
6. Vegetable masala — ½ tsp

METHOD

1. Put 30-40 ml of water in a deep pan and add tomato paste with fenugreek leaves. Let it boil and be reduced to half.
2. Add dry vegetable masala with fresh peas. Cover it and cook it for 10-12 minutes. After that remove the lid, add little more water along with paneer cut into pieces of less than ½ inch.
3. Let this mixture get boiled and when it gets reduced to half, add more along with Phool makhanas.
4. Cover it again and let it boil for 10-12 minutes.
5. Garnish it with freshly chopped coriander.
6. Delicious Shahi Korma is ready to be served with Indian bread or rice.

PULSES AND BEANS

They are categorized in the high protein legume foods. They are a rich source of proteins, carbohydrates, fats and vitamins equally. They take a long time to get cooked and retain their nutritive properties even after prolonged cooking. They can be of different types.

Whole or full pulses :	Broken or Chilka pulses:
Green (moong)	White (urad dhuli)
Black (urad whole)	Black (urad chilka)
Masar (black and red)	Beans, Rajma
Yellow (moong dhuli)	Chickpea (black and white)
	Lobhia (white beans)
	Lal lobhia

METHOD

1. Soak the pulse (beans either overnight or for at least 8-10 hrs.)
2. Put chopped onion, garlic flakes; ginger slices while they are soaked.
3. Add cloves, big cardamom and small cardamom to add flavour.
4. Pressure cook for 15-20 minutes on low flame.
5. Keep the whole (full) pulses on low flame for 25-40 minutes.

6. The pulse can be soaked overnight, or for 12-18 hrs. Then, it can be cooked in a cover pan on low flame.
7. Two-three pulses can be combined together for a good flavour. Let us have a look on the common modes for any pulse (beans to be prepared)

INGREDIENTS

1. Masala (constituting ground paste of ginger, garlic, onion and tomatoes)
2. Pulses/pulse/beans soaked.

METHOD

(1) Heat/pulse/beans in a covered pan. Once it starts cooking, add cloves, big cardamom and masala. Heat on low flame for 35-40 minutes.

(2) Garnish with coriander leaves when cooked.

ASPARAGUS

It was one of the vegetables known to Romans. It is rich in sodium, calcium, iron and sulphur. It also contains a nitrogenous principle called "asparagines" which has diuretic properties. The small, tender young shoots are more palatable then the stocks exposed to air. It has high mineral and vitamin content. Its consumption prevents or counteracts blood acidity. It should be steamed or cooked in a waterless cooker. It is steamed for 20-25 minutes and consumed either as such or with a vegetable mixture

BRUSSELS SPROUTS

They resemble miniature cabbage in appearance. They have been cultivated from wild cabbage. They are rich in minerals and vitamins. They are cooked in salted boiling water for 25-30 minutes.

CELERY

It has been a crop consumed since ancient Greek times. It was used by Greeks not as a food but also as a decorative. Among its many varieties, Celeriac is used extensively for its roots. It has a tonic effect and adds flavour to other foods. It is used mainly as a salad.

CHARD

Swiss Chard is a leafy vegetable and is used primarily for salads. The stalks and midribs are cooked but it can be consumed uncooked.

CUCUMBER

It is native to Asia and is very closely related to the watermelon, gourd and pumpkin family. It is very rich in alkaline, minerals, is refreshing and contains Vitamin A & C. It contains nearly 95% water.

GREENS

Greens include beet leaves, collards, dandelions, spinach, mustard, turnip tops, methi, chenopodium and other green leaves which are used as food in cooked form. Greens contain only a small amount of food but are valuable in the diet because of their high mineral and vitamin content. The leaves of spinach and dandelions are especially rich in iron.

Mustard greens are the leaves of the mustard plant. They may be used for salads, or can be cooked alone or in combination with vegetables. Turnip tops are the leaves of turnips and make excellent greens of good flavour. Chicory and dandelion greens can be used for salads. Spinach is rich in calcium and iron and may be eaten raw or cooked. To boil greens, place them in a pot but do not add too much water, as the water left from the waste will be sufficient to cook them. Steaming is definitely a better way.

The lettuce is used more than any other salad plant. It was cultivated by the ancient Greeks and Romans. It is rich in calcium, potassium and iron. If possible, lettuce leaves should be included in the diet at least once daily. The commonest variety is the head of the cabbage lettuce which is also known as "Romaine". The leaves of romaine are long and heavy while the head lettuce has round leaves.

METHOD

(1) Wash them thoroughly under running tap water.
(2) Cut them finely but wash them before cutting.
(3) Do not overcook them.
(4) Always prefer to cook them on low flame and in an iron karahi.

LEMON

It is a citrus fruit native to tropical and subtropical regions. It is one of the richest sources of citric acid (about 6%). It is also rich in alkaline minerals and the antiscorbutic Vitamin C. Lemon juice is widely used in healthy cooking to replace vinegar.

MUSHROOMS

They are edible fungi which grow in moist places. Some varieties of mushroom are poisonous but some of them are edible. They are used as meat substitute but they have little digestible protein and contain no vitamins. They are still considered a delicacy.

PARSLEY

It is a relative of the carrot. Its leaves are used mostly for soups and salads, and as a garnish. It contains an oil which has a distinct flavour and tonic properties.

PARSNIPS

They are related to the carrot, and though similar in form are much lighter in colour. They are usually cream coloured and have a distinct flavour. Starch is present in them in exceedingly fine granules on an average from 5 to 7%. It may be steamed; boiled or baked.

PEPPER

They belong to the same family as tomatoes. The commonest variety among them is Bell pepper which is large, green and is used as a vegetable either raw or cooked. It has a rich, hot or burning taste and is rich in vitamin C.

SWEET POTATOES

Sweet potatoes (Shakarkandi) are grown chiefly in the subtropical countries and in the warmer temperature zones. They are one of the principle root crops in Spain and Japan. It is not a tuber, as is the potato, and is not related to the vegetable. It also differs from potato since its carbohydrates include large quantities of sugar. The calorific value is the greatest per pound of any common root or any other type of vegetable.

It can be consumed either by baking or boiling.

METHOD

(1) It can be boiled or roasted or even baked.
(2) Peel it, cut into small pieces. Put salt, chat masala and lemon juice on it.
(3) It is ready to be eaten.

part 10
RAITAS

It is an indigenous part of the Indian cuisine. Raitas are an accomplice to the Indian cuisine. The base used for its preparation is curd. It has a good nutritive value with high proteins, calcium, vitamin A and vitamin K respectively.

Let us have a look on the different recipes of raita.

- Radish Raita
- Potato Raita
- Carrot, Spinach Raita
- Mint Raita
- Pumpkin Raita
- Mixed Veg Raita
- Nutty Mutty Raita
- Fruity Raita

- Boondi ka Raita
- Tomato Raita
- Chickpea Raita
- Cabbage Raita
- Eggplant Raita
- Gourd Raita
- Chenopodium Raita

POTATO RAITA

INGREDIENTS

1. Potato (medium, boiled, cut into pieces) — 1
2. Coriander leaves — A few
3. Curd (churned) — 1 cup
4. Black salt — To taste
5. Cumin powder — ¼ tsp

METHOD

(1) Churn curd and mix all the ingredients together.
(2) Garnish with coriander leaves.
(3) Serve chilled.

CARROT, SPINACH RAITA

INGREDIENTS

1. Curd (churned) — ½ cup
2. Spinach (chopped) — ½ cup
3. Carrot (chopped or grated) — 1/2
4. Green chilly (chopped) — 1
5. Cumin (Roasted) — ¼ tsp
6. Salt — To taste
7. Red chilly powder — ¼ tsp

METHOD

(1) Grate the carrot or chop it finely.

(2) Cook spinach on low flame for a few minutes. When it is cool, blend it in the mixer.

(3) Churn curd and mix all the ingredients together.

(4) Serve chilled.

MINT RAITA

INGREDIENTS

1. Curd (churned)   ½ cup
2. Mint leaves (chopped)   ¼ cup
3. Green chilly (chopped)   ½
4. Salt   To taste
5. Red chilly powder   ¼ tsp
6. Cumin seed (roasted)   ¼ tsp

METHOD

(1) Churn curd and add salt, cumin and chilly powder.

(2) Wash and grind mint leaves.

(3) Mix all the ingredients together.

(4) Serve chilled.

Note: Instead of mint, coriander leaves can also be used.

PUMPKIN RAITA

INGREDIENTS

1. Pumpkin (grated) — ¼ cup
2. Curd (churned) — ½ cup
3. Salt — To taste
4. Cumin powder — ¼ tsp

METHOD

(1) Churn curd and add salt.

(2) Grate pumpkin and steam it till it has become soft.

(3) Mix it in the curd and garnish with cumin powder.

(4) Serve chilled.

MIXED VEGETABLE RAITA

INGREDIENTS

1. Onion & tomato (small sized, chopped) — 1 each
2. Green chilly (chopped) — 1
3. Cucumber (small sized, chopped) — ½
4. Carrot (small sized, chopped) — 1
5. Curd — 1 cup
6. Coriander leaves — Few
7. Salt — To taste
8. Cumin powder — ¼ tsp

METHOD

(1) Churn curd and mix cumin powder.

(2) Add salt to the onions and keep them aside.

(3) Mix all the vegetables into the curd. Add onions in the end.

(4) Garnish with coriander leaves.

(5) Serve chilled.

NUTTY MUTTY RAITA

INGREDIENTS

1. Cashew nuts (soaked)	5-6
2. Dates	2-3
3. Kishmish	40-50 g
4. Almonds (soaked)	10-12
5. Pistachio nuts	10-12
6. Curd (churned)	1 cup
7. Cumin powder	¼ tsp

METHOD

(1) Soak all the nuts overnight. Peel the almonds and cashew nuts.

(2) Remove the seeds of dates.

(3) Churn curd and mix all the ingredients together.

(4) Sprinkle cumin powder and serve chilled.

FRUITY RAITA

INGREDIENTS

1.	Curd	1 cup
2.	Sugar	1 tsp
3.	Banana (sliced)	½
4.	Apple (cut into pieces)	½
5.	Pomegranate (shelled)	¼ cup

METHOD

(1) Churn the curd. Add sugar and mix it well.

(2) Now add fruits.

(3) Serve chilled.

BOONDI RAITA

INGREDIENTS

1. Boondi (fried tiny, gramflour balls) — 50 gm
2. Curd (churned) — 1 cup
3. Salt — To taste
4. Cumin powder — ¼ tsp

METHOD

(1) Churn curd and mix all the ingredients together.

(2) Serve chilled.

TOMATO RAITA

INGREDIENTS

1. Tomato pulp or puree — ¼ cup
2. Curd (churned) — 1 cup
3. Black salt — To taste
4. Cumin powder — ¼ tsp

METHOD

(1) Churn curd and mix all the ingredients together.
(2) Serve chilled.

CHICKPEA RAITA

INGREDIENTS

1. Chickpea (boiled) — ½ cup
2. Curd (churned) — 1 cup
3. Salt — To taste
4. Cumin powder — ¼ tsp

METHOD

(1) Boil Chickpea either black or white. Once boiled, blend it in the mixer.

(2) Churn the curd. Mix all the ingredients together.

(3) Serve chilled.

CABBAGE RAITA

INGREDIENTS

1. Cabbage (grated) — ½ cup
2. Curd (churned) — 1 cup
3. Black salt — To taste
4. Cumin powder — ¼ tsp
5. Black pepper — To taste

METHOD

(1) Grate the cabbage. Steam it for 5-10 minutes till it becomes soft.

(2) Then mix it with curd. Add all the seasonings.

(3) Serve chilled.

EGGPLANT RAITA

INGREDIENTS

1. Eggplant (small) — 1
2. Curd (churned) — 1 cup
3. Black salt — To taste
4. Black pepper — ¼ tsp
5. Cumin powder — ¼ tsp

METHOD

(1) Boil the eggplant and remove the skin. Mash it thoroughly.

(2) Churn curd and mix all the ingredients together.

(3) Serve chilled.

GOURD RAITA

INGREDIENTS

1. Gourd (Ghiya) (grated) — ½ cup
2. Curd (churned) — 1 cup
3. Black salt — To taste
4. Cumin powder — ¼ tsp
5. Black pepper — ¼ tsp

METHOD

(1) Boil the grated gourd for 5-10 minutes till it has become soft. Drain the extra water and cool it.

(2) Churn curd and mix all the ingredients together.

(3) Serve chilled.

CHENOPODIUM RAITA

INGREDIENTS

1. Chenopodium (Bathua) leaves (chopped) — ½ cup
2. Curd (churned) — 1 cup
3. Green chilly (chopped) — 1
4. Black salt — To taste
5. Cumin powder — ¼ tsp

METHOD

(1) Boil the chenopodium leaves for 5-10 minutes till it has become soft and cool it.

(2) Churn curd and mix all the ingredients together.

(3) Serve chilled.

part 11
PICKLES

Pickles are also a good accessory in the Indian diet. Although it is rich in seasonings and oil but this book presents recipes which are absolutely oil free or recipes that have a minimum use of mustard oil.

Let us have a look on the common pickles which are easy to make and easy to digest as well.

- Instant Mango Pickle
- Ginger/Chilly Pickle
- Lemon Pickle
- Indian Gooseberry Pickle
- Onion Pickle
- Pumpkin Pickle
- Yam Pickle
- Cucumber Pickle
- Lady's Finger Pickle
- Green Chilly Pickle
- Mixed Vegetable Pickle
- Ganth Cauliflower Pickle
- Potato Pickle
- Carrot Pickle
- Tamarind Pickle
- Sweet 'n' Sour Garlic

INSTANT MANGO PICKLE

INGREDIENTS

1. Mango (raw) — 2
2. Salt — To taste
3. Turmeric — ¼ tsp
4. Red chilly powder — ¼ tsp

METHOD

(1) Wash mango thoroughly and cut it into thin, long pieces.
(2) Put them in a porcelain vessel. Add salt, turmeric and chilly powder.
(3) Mix it well. Keep it covered for 2 days.
(4) Ready to use.

GINGER/CHILLY PICKLE

INGREDIENTS

1.	Ginger (cut into long pieces)	50 gm
2.	Lemon juice	3-4 tsp
3.	Salt	To taste
4.	Chilly green	4-5

METHOD

(1) Take a glass or a porcelain dish. Cut ginger into long pieces. Add lemon juice.

(2) Cut the chillies also into long pieces.

(3) Mix it with ginger, add salt.

(4) Mix it thoroughly.

(5) Keep them so for 2 days.

(6) Ready to eat.

LEMON PICKLE

INGREDIENTS

1. Small lemon — 10-15
2. Salt — To taste
3. Ajwain — 20-30 gm
4. Black salt — ¼ tsp
5. Black pepper — 1 tsp

METHOD

(1) Wash the lemon. Make cuts into them. Open up the lemons by stretching the skin.
(2) Mix all the seasonings; salt, black pepper, ajwain and black salt.
(3) Fill the lemon with this mixture.
(4) Put these lemons in a glass dish. Keep it in sunlight for 3-4 days; wait for them to become ripe.
(5) Ready to eat.

INDIAN GOOSEBERRY PICKLE

INGREDIENTS

1. Indian gooseberry (medium size) — 10-12
2. Salt — To taste
3. Red chilly powder — ¼ tsp
4. Turmeric powder — ¼ tsp

METHOD

(1) Wash the Indian gooseberry. Make cuts into them so that the fruit becomes absorbent.

(2) Mix all the ingredients with the Indian gooseberries and keep them in a glass utensil.

(3) Keep them in sunlight for 2-3 days.

(4) Indian gooseberries can be boiled before using them instead of using them raw.

(5) When ripe the pickle is ready to be consumed.

ONION PICKLE

INGREDIENTS

1. Onions (small sized) — 5-6
2. Vinegar (white) — 4-5 tsp
3. Salt — To taste

METHOD

(1) Peel the onions. Wash them and make cuts in the onions.

(2) Put vinegar in a glass bottle. Add salt and onions to it.

(3) Shake them well. Once they turn pink, the onion pickle is ready to be consumed.

PUMPKIN PICKLE

INGREDIENTS

1. Pumpkin (cut into small pieces) — ½ cup
2. Rye grains — 2-3 tsp
3. Salt — To taste
4. Turmeric powder — ¼ tsp
5. Red Chilly powder — To taste

METHOD

(1) Cut the pumpkin into small pieces.

(2) Add salt, rye granules, turmeric and chilly powder with the pumpkin pieces.

(3) Mix them well. Keep them in sunlight for 2-3 days.

(4) When ripe, the pickle is ready to be consumed.

YAM PICKLE

INGREDIENTS

1. Yam (Kachalu) — 2-3
2. Salt — To taste
3. Lemon — 2-3 tsp
4. Black pepper — ¼ tsp
5. Red chilly powder — ¼ tsp

METHOD

(1) Boil yam, peel and cut it into small pieces.

(2) Mix all the ingredients together. Keep it in sunlight for a day.

(3) The pickle is ready to be consumed.

CUCUMBER PICKLE

INGREDIENTS

1.	Cucumber (small)	5-6
2.	Red chillies	5-6
3.	Pepper corns	10-12
4.	Vinegar	1 bottle
5.	Sugar	1 cup
6.	Salt	2 tsp

METHOD

(1) Peel and cut the cucumber in halves, remove the seeds and pith. Prick the cucumber pieces with a fork, sprinkle salt on them and let them be so for a day.

(2) Make syrup with sugar and vinegar adding whole chillies and pepper corns.

(3) Now place the cucumbers in the syrup and gave them a boil, gradually adding more salt.

(4) Cool the syrup and then keep it in a bottle.

(5) The pickle is ready to use.

LADY'S FINGER PICKLE

INGREDIENTS

1.	Lady finger	15-20
2.	Green chillies (sliced)	¼ cup
3.	Ginger (shredded)	50 gm
4.	Lemon juice	20 lemons
5.	Mustard seed powder	4 tsp
6.	Salt	To taste
7.	Turmeric powder	2 tsp

METHOD

(1) Mix together salt, turmeric powder and mustard powder and keep the mixture aside.

(2) Soak whole lady finger in lime water for 10 minutes.

(3) Drain and wipe each one well.

(4) Slit lady finger length wise and stuff each one with the prepared mixture.

(5) Arrange lady finger and ginger in a jar in layers.

(6) Tie the jar with a muslin cloth and keep it in the sun for 3-4 days.

(7) Pour lime on the layers on the 5th day and keep the jar in the sun for a week. Remember to shake the jar every day.

GREEN CHILLY PICKLE

INGREDIENTS

1.	Green chilly (large)	8-10
2.	Rye seeds (powdered)	5-6 tsp
3.	Salt	To taste
4.	Turmeric powder	¼ tsp

METHOD

(1) Wash the chillies, dry them, and cut them from the middle.

(2) Powder rye seeds. Then add salt and turmeric powder to them. Fill this mixture in to the green chillies.

(3) Put them in a glass jar. Sprinkle only few drops of mustard oil over them.

(4) Keep the mixture in the sun for 5-8 days. When the mixture had become ripe, serve it with meals.

GARLIC PICKLE

INGREDIENTS

1. Garlic flakes   One ball
2. Cumin seeds   20-30 g
3. Salt   To taste
4. Black pepper   ¼ tsp

METHOD

(1) Remove the skin of garlic flakes and pat them dry.

(2) Put them in a glass jar.

(3) Roast black Cumin seeds. Mix them with the garlic flakes.

(4) Add salt and black pepper.

(5) Keep the mixture in the sun for 3-4 days.

(6) When ripe, the pickle is ready to be eaten.

MIXED VEGETABLE PICKLE

INGREDIENTS

1.	Carrots	3-4
2.	Cauliflower	1 flower
3.	Turnips	5-6
4.	Jaggery	200 gm
5.	Vinegar	250 ml
6.	Ginger (grated)	50 gm
7.	Garlic flakes	8-10
8.	Cloves	5-6
9.	Salt	To taste
10.	Red chilly powder	1 tsp
11.	Turmeric powder	1 tsp

METHOD

(1) Wash all the vegetables.
(2) Cut the vegetables into small to medium sizes.
(3) Heat water in a pan and dip the vegetables in them for 10-12 minutes.
(4) Heat jaggery in a pan, put vinegar and allow it to be there for ½ an hour.
(5) Add separately grated ginger, garlic flakes and heat them together. Then add to it cloves, salt, turmeric and chilly powder.
(6) Mix all the vegetables together in this mixture. Cook them in the pan for 15-20 minutes.
(7) When cool, add jaggery and vinegar mixture to it.
(8) Preserve it in a glass dish. Keep the mixture in the glass jar in the sun for 2 days.
(9) Ready to use.

GANTH CAULIFLOWER PICKLE

INGREDIENTS

1. Ganth Cauliflower (cut into pieces) — 2-3 flowers
2. Vinegar — 2-3 tsp
3. Salt — To taste
4. Rye powder — 5-6 tsp
5. Garam masala — ¼ tsp

METHOD

(1) Cut the ganth Cauliflower into small pieces. Dip it in vinegar for 2-3 hours.

(2) Mix salt, rye powder and garam masala with it.

(3) Put this in a glass jar. Keep it in the sun for 2 days.

(4) Ready to eat.

Note: *Garam Masala: corinander seeds, cumin seeds, black pepper corns, black cumin seeds, dry ginger powder, cardamom, cloves, cinnamon.*

POTATO PICKLE

INGREDIENTS

1.	Potatoes (raw)	5-6
2.	Rye powder	5-6 tsp
3.	Salt	To taste
4.	Black pepper seeds	10-15
5.	Black salt	To taste

METHOD

(1) Select medium size potatoes, do not remove the skin completely. Wash them. Sprinkle salt on them and keep them for 2-3 hours.

(2) Mix rye powder, salt, black pepper seeds and black salt together.

(3) Put this mixture in the glass jar and wipe the potatoes with a cloth. Add these potatoes to the jar.

(4) Keep it in sun for 5-6 days.

(5) When they turn brown, the pickle is ready to serve be served.

CARROT PICKLE

INGREDIENTS

1. Carrots (peeled) — 5-6
2. Rye seeds — 2-3 tsp
3. Salt — To taste
4. Black pepper — ¼ tsp
5. Red chilly powder — ¼ tsp
6. Turmeric powder — ¼ tsp

METHOD

(1) Peel the carrots, cut them into long pieces.

(2) Put these carrots in a glass jar. Add rye seeds, salt, black pepper, chilly and turmeric powder.

(3) Shake them well. Keep it in sun for 2-3 days. When ripe, ready to be use.

TAMARIND PICKLE

INGREDIENTS

1.	Tamarind	3 cups
2.	Jaggery	2 cups
3.	Whole red chillies	15-16
4.	Cumin seeds	3 tsp
5.	Ani seeds	3 tsp
6.	Fenugreek seeds	2 tsp
7.	Kalonji	2 tsp
8.	(Carom seeds) (Ajwain)	1 tsp
9.	Salt	To taste

METHOD

(1) Roast and powder cumin seeds and whole red chillies and keep them aside.
(2) Boil and coarsely pound aniseeds, fenugreek seeds, kalonji, carom seeds and keep them aside.
(3) Soak tamarind in 2 cups of water for sometime. Then, mash it well and force it through a strainer, with hands, to get the pulp. Discard the seeds and strings.
(4) Boil jaggery and tamarind juice and keep it on fire and boil till the liquid is reduced to half.
(5) Add salt and chilly, cumin seeds powder and cook till it has become thick.
(6) Add broken and pounded masalas and cook it for about a minute.
(7) Take it off the fire. Cool it and then preserve in a bottle.

SWEET 'N' SOUR GARLIC

INGREDIENTS

1. Garlic cloves (medium sized) — 15-20
2. Brown Sugar — 3 tsp
3. Black salt — To taste
4. Vinegar white — 3-4 tsp
5. Cumin seeds — 10 g

METHOD

(1) Take a pan. Put few drops of mustard oil in it. Once it is hot, add cumin seeds. When they get crakling, add the washed garlic cloves to it.

(2) Leave it on low flame for 2-3 minutes, covered. Put sugar and stir it well. Again cover it for 2-3 min.

(3) Once it is slightly cooked, add vinegar and salt once it has become soft.

(4) Serve hot or cool with chapatti or rice.

NOTE: This pickle is of great help to control high cholesterol and fatty liver.

part 12
DIPS

Dips are another very good accessory item in the Indian serving. Without any pickle or dip, Indian food seems incomplete. Nature has gifted us so many things which are being seasoned, and can be used as dip not only to add flavour to our food but to also make it more palatable and digestive.

Let us have a look on different types of dips.

- Coriander/Mint Dip
- Pulse Dip
- Dates Dip
- Tamarind Dip
- Coriander Dip
- Onion Dip
- Coconut Dip
- Raisin Dip
- Raw Mango Dip
- Tomato Onion Dip
- Indian Gooseberry Dip
- Garlic Dip
- Radish Dip
- Green Chilly Dip
- Plum Dip

CORIANDER/MINT DIP

INGREDIENTS

1.	Coriander Leaves	1 Cup
2.	Mint Leaves	½ cup
3.	Green Chilies	3-4
4.	Lemon Juice	2 Lemons
5.	Salt	To taste
6.	Black salt	¼ tsp
7.	Cumin seeds	½ tsp

METHOD

(1) Separate the leaves of coriander and mint.

(2) Wash them thoroughly and put them in a blender. Add green chilies.

(3) Blend them thoroughly.

(4) Add all the seasonings and mix them well again.

(5) Serve with either curd or any other snack.

(6) Sugar can be added to make it more palatable.

PULSES DIP

INGREDIENTS

1. Chickpea pulse — ½ cup
2. Urd pulse — ¼ cup
3. Curd — ½ cup
4. Salt — To taste

METHOD

(1) Dry roast the pulses separately.

(2) Then mix curd and pulses, ground them to a paste.

(3) Adjust the seasonings according to taste.

(4) Serve with bread or dhokla.

DATES DIP

INGREDIENTS

1.	Dates	¾ cup
2.	Sugar	5 tsp
3.	Vinegar	5 tsp
4.	Ginger-garlic (paste)	1 tsp
5.	Mustard seeds (paste)	½ tsp
6.	Cinnamon powder	½ cup
7.	Clove powder	½ tsp
8.	Raisins	½ cup
9.	Salt	To taste

METHOD

(1) Put sugar and vinegar in a pan and cook them over low heat till the sugar dissolves.

(2) Add all the remaining ingredients to it expect raisins.

(3) Keep stirring the mixture on low heat till it has thickened.

(4) Finally add the raisins and salt.

(5) When it has become cool store it in a jar.

TAMARIND DIP

INGREDIENTS

1. Tamarind seeds — 250 g
2. Sugar/jaggery — 150 g or ½ cup
3. Salt — To taste
4. Black pepper — ¼ tsp
5. Black salt — To taste
6. Cumin powder — ¼ tsp

METHOD

(1) Soak tamarind in water for 2-3 hrs.

(2) Then, keep the tamarind on low flame and add jaggery while on flame. But if sugar is being used add it after cooling the tamarind.

(3) Once the tamarind gets boiled, becomes thick, allow it to cool.

(4) Pass it through a fine sieve and let the liquid get separated.

(5) Collect this liquid in a pan, add sugar, salt, black pepper, Cumin powder to it and mix them well again.

(6) Once it has become thick, let it cool.

(7) It can be served with food by adding grapes, bananas, onion or even pomegranate seeds.

CORINADER DIP

INGREDIENTS

1. Chickpeas (roasted) — 1 cup
2. Mint leaves — 1 big bunch
3. Coriander leaves — 2 small bunches
4. Tamarind — 4-5 tsp
5. Green chillies — 2-4
6. Salt — To taste
7. Asafetida — Pinch

METHOD

(1) Add enough water to the tamarind pieces and soak them for 10 minutes.

(2) Then squeeze out the juice.

(3) Grind all the remaining ingredients and mix them to the tamarind pulp.

(4) Add a dash of asafetida to give it a good taste and serve it.

ONION DIP

INGREDIENTS

1. Onions (chopped) — 2 big
2. Green chillies — 3-4
3. Red chillies — 2-3
4. Ginger (cut) — 1 piece
5. Tamarind — ¼ cup
6. Salt and sugar — To taste

METHOD

(1) Grind all the ingredients together without adding water.

(2) The dip is ready to be served.

COCONUT DIP

INGREDIENTS

1.	Coconut (fresh, grated)	1 cup
2.	Rye seeds	1 tsp
3.	Curd	½ cup
4.	Green chillies	3-4
5.	Salt	To taste

METHOD

(1) Ground and grate the coconut. Mix curd to it and blend it well in the mixer.

(2) Heat a pan, add rye seeds till they start crackling. Now add the mixture of coconut and curd. Add salt and green chillies to it.

(3) Heat it for 5-7 minutes till the extra water has been soaked.

(4) Serve with idli or upma.

RAISIN DIP

INGREDIENTS

1. Raisins — ¾ cup
2. Sugar — 1 tsp
3. Chilly (red) — ¼ tsp
4. Cumin — ¼ tsp
5. Salt — To taste
6. Water — 2 cup

METHOD

(1) Mix all the ingredients and boil them on low flame.

(2) Keep on boiling till the contents are reduced to ¼ of its volume.

(3) Add more sugar and salt if necessary.

(4) Ready to serve.

RAW MANGO DIP

INGREDIENTS

1. Mango (raw, grated) — 1 cup
2. Onion (small, grated) — 2
3. Green chillies (chopped) — 2-3
4. Salt and black salt — To taste
5. Sugar — 4-5 tsp

METHOD

(1) Blend raw mango, onion and chillies in the blender.

(2) Add sugar, salt and black salt to it. Sprinkle mint leaves.

(3) Ready to serve.

TOMATO ONION DIP

INGREDIENTS

1.	Onion	2-3 big
2.	Tomatoes	4 big
3.	Green chillies	2-3
4.	Salt	To taste
5.	Mustard seeds	½ tsp
6.	Black gram pulse	1 tsp
7.	Asafetida	Pinch
8.	Curry & coriander leaves	A few

METHOD

(1) Cut onions, tomatoes and green chillies.

(2) In an iron deep pan add mustard seeds. When they pop add the pulse and cook till they turn red in colour.

(3) Add green chillies, coriander and curry leaves, cook with few drops of water.

(4) Now add onions and saute till they turn golden brown. Finally add tomatoes and salt. Cook it for few minutes.

(5) Transfer the mixture to a plate and allow it to cool.

(6) When cool, grind it in a mixer and serve.

INDIAN GOOSEBERRY DIP

INGREDIENTS

1.	Indian Gooseberry (cut into pieces)	2-3
2.	Onion (small, chopped)	1
3.	Green chillies	2-3
4.	Salt	To taste
5.	Mint leaves (dry)	Few

METHOD

(1) Mix all the ingredients together in a blender.

(2) Spread mint leaves on the mixture.

(3) Ready to serve.

GARLIC DIP

INGREDIENTS

1.	Green garlic leaves with bulb (Fresh)	3-4
2.	Green chillies	2-3
3.	Salt	To taste
4.	Mint leaves fresh	Few
5.	Pomegranate powder (Anardana)	¼ tsp

METHOD

(1) Mix all the ingredients together and blend them in a mixer.

(2) Ready to serve.

RADISH DIP

INGREDIENTS

1. Radish with leaves (large, grated) — 1
2. Green chillies — 2-3
3. Lemon juice — 1 tsp
4. Salt — To taste
5. Chat masala — ¼ tsp

METHOD

(1) Mix all the ingredients together. Blend it in a mixer.
(2) Ready to be consumed.

GREEN CHILLY DIP

INGREDIENTS

1.	Green chillies (chopped)	10-15
2.	Mustard seeds	¼ tsp
3.	Curd	¼ cup
4.	Salt	To taste

METHOD

(1) Blend chillies and mustard seeds.

(2) Add these ingredients into curd and churn it well. Add salt.

(3) Ready to serve.

PLUM DIP

INGREDIENTS

1. Plums — 6-8
2. Brown sugar — 3-4 tsp
3. Black salt — Pinch
4. Ginger essence — ½ tsp

METHOD

(1) Wash plums with peels. Soak them in water for 5-10 minutes.

(2) Take a container and add ½ cup of water and steam it for 5-7 minutes. Put the plums in the container and put them on low flame for 10 minutes.

(3) Let it cool, remove the peel, mash them and segregate the seeds. Reduce it to a pulp, add remaining sugar and salt. Keep it on low flame for 2 minutes.

(4) Once cool, add 2 drops of ginger essence.

(5) Serve with any snack or Indian bread.

part 13
CEREALS

The basic component of Indian diet is cereals which are primarily body building and energy giving foods.

The group includes wheat, rice, bajra, barley, maize, oats etc. but the prime average consumption comprises of wheat, rice and maize. Nowadays, we are coming across cases of wheat allergy especially in small kids so non cereal combinations, other than wheat should be thought of for consumption. These can be either rice, sabudana, barley, singdana ka atta or buck wheat (the typical Indian navratra food).

- Broken Wheat Pongal
- Broken Wheat Pulao
- Dahi Bhaat
- Haryali Pulao
- Mushroom Pulao
- Khichdi
- Lemon Rice
- Tamarind Rice
- Tomato Rice
- Delicious Corn flour bread

BROKEN WHEAT PONGAL

INGREDIENTS

1.	Broken wheat	2 cup
2.	Green gram pulse	½ cup
3.	Cumin seeds	½ tsp
4.	Pepper powder	A pinch
5.	Mustard seeds	¼ tsp
6.	Curry leaves	A few
7.	Salt	To taste

METHOD

(1) Steam 2 cups of broken wheat, ½ cups of water and ½ cup of green gram pulse.

(2) When done, season them with roasted cumin seeds, mustard seeds and curry leaves.

(3) Serve hot.

BROKEN WHEAT PULAO

INGREDIENTS

1.	Broken wheat (pulseia)	1 cup
2.	Vegetables (grated)	1 cup
3.	Onion (medium sized)	3
4.	Garlic	3 cloves
5.	Tomatoes (medium sized)	2
6.	Salt	To taste
7.	Mint leaves	1 bunch
8.	Lime juice	1 tsp
9.	Nutrela (granules)	¾ cup
10.	Ginger (grated)	1 piece
11.	Coriander leaves	A few
12.	Green chillies	2
13.	Water	2 cup

METHOD

(1) Grind onions, ginger, garlic and green chillies.
(2) Sauté all the ground ingredients.
(3) To this add all the vegetables, nutrella, coriander and mint leaves along with salt. Cook till done well.
(4) Dry roast pulseia separately.
(5) To this add boiling water and cook on slow fire till water dries up.
(6) Mix the cooked broken wheat with all the vegetables.
(7) Remove it from fire and add few drops of lime juice.
(8) Serve hot garnished with coriander leaves.

DAHI BHAAT

INGREDIENTS

1.	Rice (boiled in salted water)	1½ cup
2.	Milk	1 cup
3.	Curd (churned)	2 cups
4.	Red chillies	2-3
5.	Black gram pulse	1 tsp
6.	Mustard seeds	½ tsp
7.	Asafetida	A pinch
8.	Ginger (grated)	2-3 pieces
9.	Curry leaves	few
10.	Green chillies (chopped)	2
11.	Coriander leaves	Few
12.	Salt	To taste

METHOD

(1) In a pan, add red chillies, black gram pulse, asafetida, mustard seeds, ginger and curry leaves. Cook them for 12-15 mins.

(2) Take the pan off the fire and mix in the curd.

(3) Then add milk to the cooked rice and keep it for few hours before serving to get a better taste.

(4) Garnish with chopped coriander leaves.

HARIYALI PULAO

INGREDIENTS

1. Rice — 1 cup
2. Cumin seeds — 1 tsp
3. Capsicum — 1
4. Beans — 7-8
5. Fresh green peas — ½ cup
6. Coriander leaves — For garnishing

METHOD

(1) Dry roast the cumin seeds. When done add rice and cook for some time.

(2) Now add beans, fresh peas, salt and cook the ingredients in a pressure cooker for 5-7 mins.

(3) Before serving add chopped capsicum, coriander and serve hot.

MUSHROOM PULAO

INGREDIENTS

1.	Rice	2 ½ cups
2.	Mushroom (chopped)	2 cups
3.	Onions (chopped)	2
4.	Garlic (paste)	½ tsp
5.	Spring onions (chopped)	2
6.	Coriander leaves	Few
7.	Salt and pepper	To taste
8.	Chilly powder	To taste

METHOD

(1) In a pan, sauté onions, garlic paste and mushrooms.

(2) When done add rice, salt, pepper and 5-6 cups of water.

(3) Simmer on moderate heat till the water is absorbed and rice is done.

(4) Add coriander leaves and spring onions, mix well.

(5) Serve hot.

KHICHADI

INGREDIENTS

1.	Rice (soaked for ½ hour)	1 cup
2.	Bengal gram pulse	1 cup
3.	Bay leaf	1
4.	Cardamom	2
5.	Cinnamon (pulse chini)	5 cm stick
6.	Pepper corns	2-3
7.	Cumin seeds	1 tsp
8.	Salt	To taste

METHOD

(1) Boil Bengal gram pulse in water till done.

(2) Drain and keep the liquid aside.

(3) Roast the masala and add drained rice.

(4) Add water to the liquid in which Bengal gram pulse was boiled to make 2 ½ cups.

(5) Add this water to rice and give one quick boil.

(6) Now add boiled pulse to it, cover it and cook it till it is done.

(7) Serve hot.

LEMON RICE

INGREDIENTS

1. Rice — 1 cup
2. Water (double the amount of rice) — 2 cups
3. Whole red chillies — 1-2
4. Turmeric powder — ¼ tsp
5. Mustard seeds — 1 tsp
6. Salt — To taste
7. Lemon — 1

METHOD

(1) Boil the rice and cool them.

(2) Add mustard seeds in a pan, when they start popping, add whole red chillies, roast for 2 minutes.

(3) Add seasonings and rice and mix them well.

(4) Remove from heat, add lemon juice and mix well.

TAMARIND RICE

INGREDIENTS

1.	Rice	1 cup
2.	Tamarind (soaked in 1 cup of water)	
3.	Turmeric powder	½ tsp
4.	Salt	To taste
5.	Bengal gram pulse	1 tsp
6.	Mustard seeds	1 tsp
7.	Chillies	2
8.	Curry leaves	Few

FOR GROUND MASALA:

1.	Black gram pulse	1 tsp
2.	Asafetida	1 tsp
3.	Fenugreek seeds	¼ tsp

METHOD

(1) Roast and grind the dry masala to a fine powder.

(2) Boil rice and keep it aside.

(3) Roast mustard seeds, chillies and Bengal gram pulse.

(4) Add ground masala, salt, turmeric powder, tamarind water and curry leaves. Cook it for 10-12 minutes.

(5) Mix the above masala with boiled rice and serve.

TOMATO RICE

INGREDIENTS

1.	Rice	1 cup
2.	Water	Double the amount of rice
3.	Turmeric powder	¼ tsp
4.	Whole red chillies	2
5.	Tomato puree	5 tsp

METHOD

(1) Prepare the boiled rice in the usual manner.

(2) In a pan add mustard seeds, when they splinter add red chillies and immediately add tomato puree. Cook for some time. Add boiled rice and again cook for a few minutes.

(3) Mix well and serve hot.

DELICIOUS CORN FLOUR BREAD

INGREDIENTS

1.	Corn Flour (Makki)	250 gm
2.	Methi leaves fresh	50 gm
3.	Carrot or radish (grated)	100 gm
4.	Milk	¼ cup

METHOD

(1) Mix all the ingredients together in a bowl except milk.

(2) Since all the ingredients have enough moisture, add milk slowly to make a soft dough.

(3) Knead it softly and make round balls.

(4) Take a Indian bread maker and switch it on.

(5) Keep the round balls and press it. Once it is brown, turn to other side till brown.

(6). Serve hot with Dip or sarson ka saag.

part 14
SWEET DISHES

What would you like to have after dinner/lunch? The usual question asked by your host and often by you too.

The most wanted item after dinner or lunch which gives a feeling of fullness, digestion & satisfaction after any meals is a sweet dish.

They are of different types with different colourful values. They can be cooked with a medium of oil/ghee or without it.

Always use brown sugar so that the calorific value is minimum. Enjoy the platter of many enjoyable sweet dishes which can be easily prepared at home.

- Rice Pudding
- Sago Pudding
- Cocoa Rolls
- Vermicelli Pudding
- Khoya Rolls
- Kesari Raj Bhog
- Mango Ice-Cream
- Custard with Jelly
- Shahi Tukra
- Nutty Mutty
- Fruit Crush
- Strawberry Phirni
- Shrikhand
- Modak
- Semolina Coconut Ladoo
- Fruit Cream
- Coconut Pudding
- Cardamom Fudge
- Gramflour Ladoo
- Carrot Pudding
- Sweet Pulse and Rice
- Gourd Burfi
- Moong Pulse Ka Halwa
- Pulse-E-Pudding
- Pumpkin Halwa
- Orange Spiced
- Stuffed Pears
- Dates Flour
- Gulab Jamun
- Sweet Rice
- Dates Pudding
- Sponge Rasgula
- Anjeer Ki Burfi
- Rabri Faluda
- Rasmalai
- Semolina Pudding
- Gramflour Halwa
- Sandesh
- Carrot Halwa
- Kulfi
- Sweetened Curd
- Apple Snowballs
- Coco Khoya
- Potato Halwa
- Chocopie

RICE PUDDING

INGREDIENTS

1. Rice — 200 g
2. Milk toned — 500 ml
3. Sugar — 4 tsp
4. Almonds (roasted) — 4-5
5. Cardamom — 1

METHOD

(1) Soak rice overnight along with almonds.
(2) Bring milk to boil and heat it on low flame for 20-25 minutes till it starts thickening.
(3) Add rice and let it to be on flame with the lid covered.
(4) Add sugar and cardamom.
(5) Serve hot.

SAGO PUDDING

INGREDIENTS

1.	Sago (Sabudana)	100 gm
2.	Milk	200 ml
3.	Sugar	3 tsp
4.	Soaked walnut	2

METHOD

(1) Soak sago for 35-40 min.

(2) Boil milk. Add sago to it when it comes to boil. Keep it on low flame for 10 min till it thickens.

(3) Peel the walnuts. Cut them into small pieces and garnish.

(4) Serve hot / cold.

COCOA ROLLS

INGREDIENTS

1.	Milk biscuits	8-10
2.	Sugar powder	2 tsp
3.	A plastic roll	(small)
4.	Coffee powder	1 tsp
5.	Cocoa powder	1 tsp
6.	Corn flour	2 tsp
7.	Milk	5-6 tsp

METHOD

(1) Arrange biscuits together in a roll in a foil.

(2) Mix cocoa powder, coffee, sugar and corn flour. Make a thick paste with milk.

(3) Hold the biscuits together in a roll and apply the paste on both sides with a butter knife.

(4) Roll this on a plastic sheer and keep it in the freezer for 30 min.

(5) Remove the plastic sheet and cut this into rolls.

(6) Serve with either tea or as a sweet dish itself.

VERMICELLI PUDDING

INGREDIENTS

1.	Vermicelli	50g
2.	Milk toned	150 ml
3.	Sugar	3 tsp
4.	Almonds (soaked overnight)	5-6
5.	Cardamom powder	¼ tsp

METHOD

(1) Boil vermicelli in water on low flame for 10 min.

(2) Then wash it under running tap water and keep it aside.

(3) Boil milk and add cardamom powder to it. Heat it on low flame for 10 min. Add vermicelli and sugar together.

(4) Keep on heating it for 2-3 minutes. Allow it to cool.

(5) Chop the almonds and keep the Pudding in the refrigerator.

(6) Garnish with almonds and serve chilled.

KHOYA ROLLS

INGREDIENTS

1.	Paneer	50g
2.	Khoya	50g
3.	Cardamom powder	1 tsp
4.	Sugar powder	4 tsp
5.	Almonds (soaked, grated)	5-6
6.	Kewra	1 tsp

METHOD

(1) Take home made paneer. Crush it and make a thin batter. Make fine dough by gentle rubbing.

(2) Crush khoya and mix it with paneer. Dough it softly.

(3) Add sugar and cardamom powder to the dough.

(4) Mix it thoroughly and make round or oval balls.

(5) Sprinkle cut almonds on them and keep them it in the fridge for 35-40 min.

(6) Spray kewra water and serve cool.

KESARI RAJ BHOG

INGREDIENTS

1.	Paneer (From toned milk)	250 g
2.	Refined flour	1 tsp
3.	Semolina (Semolina)	1 tsp
4.	Pistachio nuts	12-15
5.	Almonds	6-8
6.	Khoya (grated)	3 tsp
7.	Green cardamom powder	1-2 tsp
8.	Rose syrup	2 tsp
9.	Sugar	4-5
10.	Saffron (kesar)	½ tsp

METHOD

(1) Take fresh paneer, knead it well until it has become smooth.
(2) Add refined flour and semolina to it and knead it gently. Divide into 12-14 equal portions.
(3) Soak pistachio nuts and almonds in one cup boiling water for five minutes. Drain, cool, peel and chop them roughly.
(4) Combine grated khoya with green cardamom powder and rose syrup. Knead it into a dough. Mix the roughly chopped, pistachio nuts and almonds to it. Divide the dough into equal twelve to fourteen portions.
(5) Stuff a portion of khoya into each portion of paneer and make marble sized balls.
(6) Combine sugar with three-four litre water. Bring it to a boil and make thin sugar syrup. Remove any impurity by passing it through a muslin cloth.
(7) When the sugar syrup has come to a boil, add saffron. Gently slide in the paneer balls and cook for four to five minutes on high heat.
(8) Sprinkle about quarter cup hot water and continue to cook on high heat for around five minutes or till they alone dribble in the side. Remove and keep in sufficient quantity of saffron infused sugar syrup.
(9) Refrigerate and serve chilled.

MANGO ICE CREAM

INGREDIENTS

1. Milk toned — 250 ml
2. Sugar — 4 tbsp
3. Custard powder — 1 tsp
4. Mango (medium, mashed thoroughly) — 1
5. Cardamom powder — ¼ tsp

METHOD

(1) Boil milk in a pan and add cardamom powder to it.
(2) Keep it on low flame and add custard powder and sugar.
(3) Keep it for 10-15 min on slow flame or till it becomes a thick syrup.
(4) Allow it to cool. Add crushed mangoes. Stir them thoroughly.
(5) Keep it in the freezer and serve chilled. Instead of mango, any seasonal fruit can also be used.

CUSTARD WITH JELLY

INGREDIENTS

1. Milk toned — 200 ml
2. Custard powder — 2 tsp
3. Jelly crystals — ½ packet
4. Sugar — 1 tbsp

METHOD

(1) Boil ¾ of milk on a low flame. When boiled add sugar.

(2) Take the remainder of the milk and mix it with custard powder. Stir it thoroughly and add it to the boiling milk.

(3) Stir thoroughly till the milk and custard mixture thickens.

(4) Cool it and set it in the refrigerator.

(5) Take jelly crystals, put them in 1 cup of warm water. Stir them thoroughly and keep in the refrigerator till they are set.

(6) Serve cool with chilled custard.

(7) To make it more delicious. Serve with fresh fruits.

SHAHI TUKRA

INGREDIENTS

1. Bread slices — 2
2. Sugar — 2
3. Cheese — 50g
4. Water — ½ litre
5. Pistachio powder — 2 tsp

METHOD

(1) Cut bread into equal square slices.

(2) Roast them on low flame and let them turn brown and then take them off the flame.

(3) Boil water and add sugar. Let it become a thick syrup.

(4) Knead the cheese thoroughly and add pistachio powder.

(5) Take the slices and dip them in the sugar solution.

(6) Arrange them in a plate, garnish with pistachio and cheese powder.

(7) Serve hot.

NUTTY MUTTY

INGREDIENTS

1. Almonds (soaked) — 15-20
2. Pistachio powder (crushed) — 2 tsp
3. Raisins (soaked) — 15-20
4. Walnut (soaked, crushed) — 5-6
5. Sugar — 2 tbsp
6. Semolina — 50g
7. Gramflour — 2 tsp
8. Milk — 50 ml

METHOD

(1) Heat milk in a pan. Roast Semolina and gramflour separately. Add them to the hot milk.

(2) Allow it to simmer on low heat. Add sugar while it is being heated.

(3) Allow it to cool and add all the crushed nuts.

(4) Put it in a container and refrigerate it.

(5) Cut into different sizes before serving.

FRUIT CRUSH

INGREDIENTS

1.	Ice-cream (vanilla)	50g
2.	Ice-cream (strawberry)	50g
3.	Pineapple (sliced)	200g
4.	Strawberry (chopped)	Few
5.	Pomegranate (small, grains)	1
6.	Soda water	1 bottle
7.	Rose water	¼ tsp

METHOD

(1) Mix all the ice-creams and add soda water to it.

(2) Churn it in a mixer.

(3) Add all the chopped fruits.

(4) Mix them thoroughly and churn lightly.

(5) Serve chilled, sprinkle rose water for flavour.

STRAWBERRY PHIRNI

INGREDIENTS

1. Rice — 4 tbsp
2. Milk — 1 litre
3. Sugar — ¾ cup
4. Fresh strawberries — 12-15
5. Pistachio nuts — 8-10
6. Almonds — 6-8

METHOD

(1) Clean, wash and soak rice in sufficient water for half an hour. Drain and grind the soaked rice to a coarse paste. Dilute rice paste with half cup of water. Wash and finely chop the remaining rice.

(2) Soak pistachio nut and almonds in hot water for five minutes, drain, peel and finely slice them.

(3) Heat milk and bring it to a boil. Gradually stir in the rice paste, reduce the heat and simmer for 3-4 minutes, stirring continuously, or till the milk has thickened.

(4) Add sugar, cardamom powder and continue to simmer till the sugar dissolves. Remove from heat. Cool it at room temperature and put in the chopped strawberries.

(5) Pour this mixture into earthen wave or ceramic bowls, garnish with sliced pistachio nuts, sliced strawberries and serve chilled.

SHRIKHAND

INGREDIENTS

1.	Yoghurt	3 cups
2.	Powdered sugar	2 ½ cups
3.	Pistachio nuts	8-10
4.	Chironji	2 tsp
5.	Saffron	A pinch
6.	Warm milk	2 tsp
7.	Green cardamom powder	½ tsp

METHOD

(1) Tie yoghurt in a muslin cloth and hang it overnight, to drain out whey. This should preferably be kept in the refrigerator.

(2) Transfer the hung yoghurt into a bowl. Add powdered sugar and mix well till sugar dissolves completely.

(3) Soak pistachio nuts in hot water for 5-10 min, drain, peel and slice them. Clean, wash and pat dry chironji.

(4) Dissolve saffron in a little warm milk and add to the yoghurt mixture. Mix well.

(5) Add chironji, green cardamom powder and mix well. Serve chilled with pistachio nuts.

MODAK

INGREDIENTS

1. Parboiled rice — 1 ½ cup
2. Salt — A pinch
3. Pure ghee — ½ tsp
4. Jaggery (grated) — ¾ cup
5. Green cardamom powder — pinch

FOR STUFFING

1. Fresh coconut (scarped) — 1 ½ cup

METHOD

(1) Clean, wash and drain rice thoroughly. Dry completely by spreading it on an absorbent sheet of cloth. Grind dried rice to a fine powder. Pass it through a fine sieve.

(2) Bring one and a quarter cups water to a boil in a pan, add salt and ghee to it.

(3) Add to it rice flour in a flow, stirring continuously to prevent lumps from forming. Remove the pan from heat and keep it covered for 10-15 min.

(4) Grease your palms with a little oil and knead the cooked rice mixture to soft dough. Keep it covered with a moist cloth.

(5) Combine scraped coconut and jaggery in a pan. Heat for 1-2 min. or till they turn light golden brown. Ensure that it is not overcooked. Add green cardamom powder and remove it from heat. Let it cool slightly. Divide the coconut mixture into 10-12 equal sized portions.

(6) Divide the rice dough into 10-12 lemon sized balls with greased palms. Press each ball in the middle to form discs with a diameter of 3 inches. Press the edge of the disc further to reduce the thickness.

(7) Place the portion of coconut and jaggery mixture in the centre of the discs. Form 8-10 pleats with finger, gather them together to form a bundle and seal the edges at the top.

(8) Steam them in an idli steamer for 10—12 min. Serve hot modak.

SEMOLINA COCONUT LADOO

INGREDIENTS

1. Milk — 50 ml
2. Semolina (Rava) — 1 ½ cup
3. Fresh coconut (scraped) — ¾ cup
4. Sugar — 1 cup
5. Raisins — 1 cup
6. Green cardamom powder — ½ tsp

METHOD

(1) Heat milk in a thick bottom pan. Stir and add, roast semolina on a very low flame, till it just starts changing colour to light golden. Add scraped coconut and continue to stir for 1-2 minutes.

(2) Cook sugar with half a cup of water on medium heat, stirring continuously till it dissolves. Increase heat and bring the syrup to a boil. Cook without stirring for about five minutes or till it reaches single thread consistency.

(3) Add the warm roasted semolina mixture and green cardamom powder to the sugar syrup and mix well. Cover the mixture with a lid and keep it aside for 30 minutes, stirring the mixture at regular intervals.

(4) Divide the mixture into 12-15 equal portions, and make it into firm ladoos by rolling them with your hands and decorate with raisins.

FRUIT CREAM

INGREDIENTS

1.	Fruits-apple, oranges, bananas (medium sized, cut into small pieces)	1 each
2.	Cardamom	1
3.	Milk toned	200 ml
4.	Sugar	2 tsp
5.	Corn flour	2-3 tsp

METHOD

(1) For fruit cream use either low fat cream or corn flour half tbs.

(2) Mix corn flour and sugar with milk.

(3) Churn it in a blender, so that it becomes thick.

(4) Add cardamom and mix all fruits.

(5) Serve chilled.

COCONUT PUDDING

INGREDIENTS

1.	Coconut (fresh, grated)	200 g/1 cup
2.	Sugar powder	50 g
3.	Milk	200 ml
4.	Cardamom powder	1 tsp
5.	Kewra	1 tsp
6.	Pistachio (soaked)	Few
7.	Walnut (soaked)	Few
8.	Almonds	Few

METHOD

(1) Peel the coconut and grate it.

(2) Soak the coconut in 50 ml of milk. Add cardamom powder in it. Keep it for 2-3 hrs.

(3) Bring milk to boil and add all the soaked nuts finely chopped into it.

(4) Ground the mixture of coconut and milk to a paste in a blender.

(5) Add this to the milk, to make a paste in a blender.

(6) Add kewra and serve chilled.

CARDAMOM FUDGE

INGREDIENTS

1. Curd — 1 ½ cup
2. Cheese (paneer) — 1 ½ cup
3. Chopped nuts — 1 tsp
4. Sugar (ground) — 7-8 tsp
5. Cardamom milk powder — 2 tsp

METHOD

(1) Hang the curd in a muslin cloth or put it into a fine mesh strainer for 2 hour or till all the water has drained out.

(2) Put the drained curd into a blender with the paneer fresh (home made) and sugar. Blend them smooth and pour them into a greased shallow dish. Sprinkle the cardamom and nuts on the mixture.

(3) At 100°F power, microwave it for 7 min, stirring only once after 2 minutes. Allow it to stand for 3-4 minutes. Cool and cut into squares.

GRAMFLOUR LADOO

INGREDIENTS

1.	Bengal gram flour	1 cup
2.	Semolina (Sooji)	¼ cup
3.	Turmeric	pinch
4.	Green cardamom	2-3

METHOD

(1) Make a syrup of sugar (½ tsp) and water (1 cup)

(2) Dry roast Bengal gram flour, gramflour and semolina in a pan on slow fire till it turns light brown.

(3) Stir constantly till the mixture emits a characteristic flavour.

(4) Remove from fire. Add turmeric and powdered cardamom and let it cool slightly.

(5) Add sugar syrup to the above mixture.

(6) Form into ladoos and serve.

CARROT PUDDING

INGREDIENTS

1.	Carrots (fresh, red, small sized)	2-3
2.	Sugar	3 tbsp
3.	Milk (Skimmed)	1 cup
4.	Green cardamom	2-3
5.	Raisins	4-5

METHOD

(1) Wash the carrots and grate them finely.

(2) Boil milk and carrots and simmer them on slow fire for 15-20 minutes with occasional stirring till the Pudding thickens.

(3) Add sugar and stir till it has dissolved.

(4) Remove it from fire. Add crushed, green cardamom.

(5) Serve hot or cold garnished with raisins.

SWEET PULSE AND RICE

INGREDIENTS

1. Rice — 1 cup
2. Jaggery — ½ cup
3. Chickpea pulse — 4 tsp
4. Water — double the volume of rice

METHOD

(1) Clean and soak the rice.
(2) Wash and cook the pulse with little water till it is tender.
(3) Cook rice in one volume of water.
(4) Make syrup of jaggery in another volume of water.
(5) Add pulse and syrup to rice and cook on low heat till the water has dried.
(6) Serve hot.

GOURD BURFI

INGREDIENTS

1. Bottle gourd (grated) — ¼ cup
2. Sugar — 1/3 cup
3. Milk (skimmed) — 1 cup
4. Kewra essence — 1-2 drops
5. Food colour (green) — few drops

METHOD

(1) Wash, peel and grate the bottle gourd.

(2) Cook the grated bottle gourd in a pan with little water till it has become tender.

(3) Add sugar and cook it with constant stirring till the mixture has thickened.

(4) Add milk to the bottle gourd mixture and cook till the mixture has left the sides of the pan.

(5) Remove from fire and add colour essence.

(6) Cover a plate with butter paper and spread the mixture on it. Cut it into pieces when set and serve.

MOONG PULSE HALWA

INGREDIENTS

1.	Moong pulse (green)	200g
2.	Semolina (Semolina)	50g
3.	Milk toned	1 cup
4.	Sugar (powdered)	6-8 tsp
5.	Pistachio	5-6
6.	Raisins	4-5
7.	Almonds (soaked)	5-6

METHOD

(1) Ground the pulse into a fine powder.

(2) Heat milk in a pan. Add Semolina and roast it on flame. Once it changes its colour, add the pulse powder and roast it on low flame for 20-25 min.

(3) Once you get a characteristic flavour, add sugar and finally chopped nuts.

(4) Serve it hot.

PULSE-E-PUDDING

INGREDIENTS

1. Green gram pulse (washed) — 1 tsp
2. Sugar — 2 tsp
3. Milk (skimmed) — 1 cup
4. Green cardamom — 1-2
5. Raisins — 4-5

METHOD

(1) Clean and soak the pulse.
(2) Boil the pulse till it gets tender.
(3) Add milk and simmer on low flame for 15-20 minutes with frequent stirring.
(4) Add sugar and stir till it gets dissolved.
(5) Remove from fire, add crushed green cardamom.
(6) Serve either hot or cold garnished with raisins.

PUMPKIN HALWA

INGREDIENTS

1. Yellow pumpkin (petha)   2 cup
2. Sugar   1 cup
3. Dates   4-5

METHOD

(1) Cook yellow pumpkin in water.

(2) When soft, add sugar to it and keep cooking till the water has dried.

(3) Finally before serving garnish with dates, and raisins.

(4) Serve either hot or cold.

ORANGE SPICED

INGREDIENTS

1.	Orange	2
2.	Orange juice	1 cup
3.	Sugar	2 ½ tsp
4.	Cloves	10-12
5.	Pepper corns	½ tsp
6.	Cardamom	6
7.	Cinnamon	2
8.	Lemon juice	2 tsp
9.	Corn starch	1 tsp

METHOD

(1) Add cloves, pepper, cardamom, cinnamon, sugar, lemon juice, corn starch and 2 cups of water in a pan.

(2) Bring it to a boil, cover and simmer till almost the entire liquid has evaporated and big bubbles have started to appear.

(3) Remove the orange peel and pith, slice it to round pieces about ¼ inch thick.

(4) To serve, bring the orange slices to a descent boil. Top each with spiced syrup and serve chilled.

STUFFED PEARS

INGREDIENTS

1. Pears (large) — 6
2. Black grapes — ¼ cup
3. Curd — 1 cup
4. Sugar — 1 tsp
5. Salt, black pepper — To taste

METHOD

(1) Tie the curd in a thin muslin cloth to drain away the extra water (at least for 3 hours)

(2) Peel the pear and cut them into 2 halves. Scoop out the inner parts.

(3) Cut the grapes and take out the seeds if any.

(4) Add sugar and salt to the curd.

(5) Put this mixture of grapes and curd into each pear cup.

(6) Serve chilled.

DATES FLOUR

INGREDIENTS

1. Fresh dates (chopped) — 2 cups
2. Wheat flour — 2 tsp
3. Big cardamom — 12 pieces

METHOD

(1) Deseed the dates and chop them into pieces.

(2) Dry roast the wheat flour.

(3) Powder the big cardamom.

(4) Mix all the three things together. Divide this mixture into equal portions.

(5) Wet your hands with a little warm milk and make small ladoos.

(6) Serve hot.

GULAB JAMUN

INGREDIENTS

1.	Flour (white flour)	100g
2.	Sugar (powdered)	50g
3.	Almonds (soaked, peeled)	5-6
4.	Pistachio powder	2 tsp
5.	Water	1 litre
6.	Corn flour	1 tsp
7.	Baking powder	¼ tsp
8.	Milk	50 ml

METHOD

(1) Add white flour, milk and baking powder in a pan.
(2) Then knead it into a soft dough. Keep it aside for 1 ½ hrs.
(3) Bring water to a boil, adding sugar into it. The sugar syrup should be thick.
(4) Mix corn flour and all the nuts.
(5) With the prepared dough make medium sized balls. Fill it with the mixture of corn flour and nuts.
(6) Heat it in a microwave oven for 4-5 min on 100 % powder, till they become light brown.
(7) Dip them in the sugar syrup, till they absorb it.
(8) Serve hot as a light sweet in the evening.

SWEET RICE

INGREDIENTS

1.	Rice	100g
2.	Jaggery	50g
3.	Milk toned	100ml
4.	Cardamom powder	1 tsp
5.	Almonds (soaked)	5-6

METHOD

(1) Soak rice for 1 ½ hrs.

(2) Boil the rice in an open container.

(3) While heating, add crushed jaggery and cardamom powder, and stir gradually so that it mixes thoroughly.

(4) Boil the milk and put it in a pan. Add the mixture of rice, jaggery and cardamom. Mix it thoroughly.

(5) Serve it either hot or cool dressed up with almonds.

DATES PUDDING

INGREDIENTS

1. Dates (chopped) — 100g
2. Milk toned — 100g
3. Cardamom powder — ¼ tsp
4. Sugar powder — 6-8 tsp
5. Rose essence — 5-6 drops
6. Corn flour — 1 tsp
7. Sago (Sabudana) — 50g

METHOD

(1) Bring milk to a boil and keep it on low flame. Add corn flour and cardamom powder.

(2) Soak sago for 30 minutes. Drain it and add it to the boiled milk.

(3) Cover it and stir it gently on low flame.

(4) When the mixture has thickened add dates and sugar.

(5) Let it cool. Then add few drop of rose essence.

(6) Serve chilled.

SPONGE RASGULA

INGREDIENTS

1. Flour (white flour) — 100g
2. Sugar powder (refined) — 10-12 tsp
3. Soda bicarbonate — ¼ tsp
4. Fresh paneer (cottage) — 100g
5. Water — 1 litre
6. Corn flour — 1 tsp

METHOD

(1) Sieve flour and corn flour.

(2) Dough paneer thoroughly so that it has become quite soft.

(3) Mix corn flour, kneaded cheese, flour together and role it into small balls.

(4) Boil water and add sugar, till it has become thick.

(5) Let it cool. Add the paneer balls. Keep them till they soak the sugar solution.

(6) Refrigerate them and serve chilled.

ANJEER KI BURFI

INGREDIENTS

1. Anjeer (figs) — 50g
2. Gur/jaggery — 100g
3. Nuts almonds and walnuts (soaked) — 50g each
4. Gramflour powder — 2-3 tsp

METHOD

(1) Soak anjeer overnight. Drain it and ground it to a fine paste.

(2) Heat jaggery in a pan till it melts. While on the flame, add gramflour and stir it gradually till it has become thick.

(3) Add anjeer and crushed walnuts and almonds.

(4) Stir it gradually while on flame, till it has become thick.

(5) Allow it to cool and cut it into pieces.

(6) In summers it can be served as such. In winter, it can be slightly heated to have a better taste.

RABRI FALUDA

INGREDIENTS

1. Milk toned — 1 litre
2. Saffron leaves — few
3. Sugar — 50g
4. Kewra (screw pine flower extract) — 1 tsp
5. Vermicelli — 50g
6. Cardamom powder — 1 tsp

METHOD

(1) Put milk in a pan with water in the pan, so that it does not stick to the pan or take a thick bottomed pan. Keep it on flame. Allow it to boil. Add saffron leaves and cardamom powder.
(2) Keep on stirring constantly so that the milk does not get burnt. Scratch the sides and bottom of the pan constantly so that the light layer of milk gets removed from the pan.
(3) When it is reduced to half, add sugar. Keep on heating on low flame, till it has become thick.
(4) Boil vermicelli in water.
(5) Strain it and wash it under running water.
(6) Put kewra essence in cold water and dip the vermicelli into it for ½-1 hr.
(7) Now take out the solid rabri. Serve it hot as such, or cool with faluda.
(8) Refrigerate it and serve chilled.

RASMALAI

INGREDIENTS

1.	Flour (white flour)	50g
2.	Sugar	50g
3.	Corn flour	1 tsp
4.	Milk	250gm
5.	Soda bicarbonate	¼ tsp
6.	Saffron leaves	few
7.	Cardamom powder	1 tsp

METHOD

(1) Mix flour, corn flour and soda bicarbonate together and make dough by thoroughly kneading it.

(2) Boil milk in an open pan. While boiling add saffron leaves and cardamom powder. Keep it on low flame till it becomes thick. Add sugar once it has cooled.

(3) Make small balls of the dough and keep it aside.

(4) Put milk in the refrigerator with the balls.

(5) Serve it chilled.

SEMOLINA PUDDING

Since time immemorial it has been a basic baby food, the most easiest, digestible and palatable food for a new born.

INGREDIENTS

1. Semolina (Rava) — 50 g
2. Sugar — 3 tsp
3. Milk toned — 100 ml
4. Cashew nuts (roasted, crushed) — 5-6
5. Urd pulse (powdered, roasted) — 50 g

METHOD

(1) Roast semolina and urd pulse separately and mix them together in the pan.//
(2) Boil milk and add sugar.
(3) Add boiled milk to the roasted ingredients and allow it to become thick.
(4) Serve hot, garnished with cashew nuts.

GRAMFLOUR HALWA

Halwa always implies a preparation of ghee and rich foods. But it is also a part of oil free recipes.

INGREDIENTS

1.	Gramflour	100g
2.	Sugar (powder)	3-4 tsp
3.	Almonds (soaked, grated)	5-6
4.	Condensed milk/toned milk	100 ml

METHOD

(1) Heat half of the milk in the pan. Add sugar and gramflour. Allow it to heat on low flame, uncovered for 15-20 min.

(2) Once it gets thick, add the remaining milk. Bring it to a boil and add grated almonds.

(3) Serve hot.

SANDESH

INGREDIENTS

1.	Pistachio nuts	8-10
2.	Almonds	10-12
3.	Saffron	few leaves
4.	Warm milk	1 tsp
5.	Paneer fresh	400g
6.	Sugar powder	½ tsp
7.	Cardamom powder	½ tsp

METHOD

(1) Soak pistachio nuts and almonds in one cup water for 10 min. Peel and chop pistachio nuts and almonds. Lightly crush and dissolve saffron in warm milk. Mix chopped pistachio nuts in milk and saffron mixture.

(2) Knead paneer with your palm to ensure that it is quite smooth in texture. Add powdered sugar and cardamom powder and knead them well.

(3) Transfer this mixture to a deep pan and cook in low flame for 4-6 minutes stirring continuously. Remove from fire, mix gently till it is cool enough to handle.

(4) Mix chopped almonds and divide into 20 equal portions.

(5) Form each portion into a desired shape, garnish with chopped pistachio nuts and soaked saffron.

(6) Chill thoroughly and serve.

CARROT HALWA

INGREDIENTS

1. Carrots (grated)   8-10
2. Skimmed milk   250 ml
3. Cardamom   2
4. Brown sugar   4-5 tsp

METHOD

(1) Take an aluminium deep pan and put milk on boil on covered flame.

(2) Once milk starts boiling put cardamom and grated carrots, heat it for 30-40 minutes till the mixture becomes semi soft.

(3) Keep on simmering in between so that it does not burn.

(4) Once the mixture starts drying & becomes soft, add sugar and stir for 5-7 minutes on low flame till the left water dries out.

(5) Serve it hot sprinkled with cashew nut & almonds as per your requirement.

KULFI

INGREDIENTS :

1. Toned/double toned milk 500 gm
2. Brown sugar 50 gm
3. Cardamom 2
4. Nuts Few

(Almonds, walnuts and raisins crushed preferably soaked)

METHOD

(1) Take a copper pan or a heavy base utensil. Keep milk for boiling on low flame, covered.

(2) Put 2 pieces of cardamom & observe till the milk boils.

(3) Keep it covered on low flame & let it boil for at least 25-30 minutes till it becomes thick.

(4) Once it has become cool, add sugar and all the nuts. Stir it slowly & allow it to cool.

(5) Take a container, grease it with few drops of oil and put the cool mixture into the container.

(6) Keep this in the chiller section of the refrigerator. Allow it to freeze.

(7) Take it out after 4-5 hrs cut into multiple pieces. Serve as it is or with fruits.

SWEETENED CURD

INGREDIENTS

1. Milk toned — 500 ml
2. Curd — 1 ½ tsp
3. Brown sugar — 50 g

METHOD

(1) Bring milk to boil. Then pour it into a microwave safe bowl. Microwave at 100 % power for 10 minutes, stirring twice.

(2) If your bowl is not deep enough, then cook on a lower power level for some more time.

(3) Add sugar to the milk and microwave for 1 more minute or slightly boil it. Stand 10 minutes or till the milk is lukewarm. Brown sugar is used only to give the characteristic colour, otherwise white sugar can also be used.

(4) In a bowl, smear the curd. Pour in the milk, stirring constantly. Leave to serve.

(5) Serve chilled.

APPLE SNOWBALLS

INGREDIENTS

1.	Apples (red, bright)	3-4
2.	Sugar	5 tsp
3.	Strawberry jam	2 tsp
4.	Egg white	2 tsp
5.	Castor sugar	2 tsp
6.	Glace cherries	3 - 4

METHOD

(1) Peel the apples and scoop out the cores to make them hollow.

(2) Dissolve granulated sugar in water and gently stew the apples.

(3) Drain apples and arrange in a baking dish greased with little curd.

(4) Fill the cavity of apples with jam.

(5) Whisk egg white and stir it. Add castor sugar and continue to stir till no sugar has remained.

(6) Pour this mixture over the apples.

(7) Bake at 300°F till light brown at the tips.

(8) Serve with glaced cherries and serve.

COCO KHOYA

INGREDIENTS

1.	Coconut (Grated)	100 gm
2.	Khoya fresh	100 gm
3.	Brown sugar	50 gm
4.	Cardamom (crushed)	2 pieces
5.	Milk	2-3 tsp

METHOD

(1) Take a clean container preferably of glass. Mash khoya till it becomes soft.

(2) Add milk and crushed seeds of cardamom with brown sugar. Again mash it softly.

(3) Leave it for 10 minutes. Then, add grated coconut and make small balls of round shape.

(4) Dress them in a plate to be served after dinner or lunch.

POTATO HALWA

INGREDIENTS

1.	Potatoes (Boiled)	3-4 medium size
2.	Brown sugar	5 tsp
3.	Milk toned	½ litre
4.	Cardamom	2

METHOD

(1) Take an aluminium pan and add 2-3 tsp of water and milk. Keep it on low flame to boil covered.

(2) Once it starts boiling add cardamom and let it boil until the milk has reduced to half.

(3) Put mashed potatoes to the mixture and stir it constantly to make semi-solid platter.

(4) Once it cools down, add brown sugar. Mix it thoroughly and serve hot.

NOTE: It is a wonderful low calorie sweet dish.

CHOCOPIE

INGREDIENTS

1.	Circular slices of bread	6-8
2.	Chocolate powder	2-3 tsp
3.	Brown sugar	4 tsp
4.	Cream (skimmed)	4-6 tsp

METHOD

(1) Cut the slices of bread in a circle.

(2) Mix chocolate powder, sugar and cream to make a batter.

(3) Arrange this batter on each slice and stick one on the other to make circular rolls.

(4) Keep it in the chiller for 5-7 minutes.

(5) Cut them into semi-circular shapes.

(6) Serve this wonderful sweet dish.

part 15
FEW HEALTH TIPS

1. Take your meals on time.
2. Take 2 glasses of water daily on empty stomach.
3. Take at least one fruit meal in a day.
4. Go for regular morning and evening walks.
5. Chew your food properly and give proper time to your stomach for digestion.
6. For a good stomach take boiled / fat free foods.
7. Avoid pulses, take good amount of salads and roughage.
8. For good skin, take one Indian gooseberry daily and eat plenty of leafy vegetables.
9. Take steam at least once a day (Nasal).
10. Do not use soap too frequently. Either use milk or gramflour.
11. For good hairs, do not change the shampoo frequently.
12. Treat and correct the dandruff efficiently.
13. Proper care of your teeth and gums is essential. Chew your food thoroughly.
14. Take plenty of Vitamin C which includes Indian gooseberry, cabbage, citrus fruits.
15. Rub your gums gently with a powder of salt, alum, and baking powder, powdered equally.
16. Do not change your toothpaste too often.
17. For respiratory system, take long, deep breaths in the morning.
18. Prefer to lie on your right side.
19. Take steam every alternate day.
20. Jal neti and sutra neti equally help in combating secretions.
21. Take 2 leaves of tulsi daily.
22. Swallow 2 cloves of garlic everyday with water.

GLOSSARY

A
Apple Pudding
Asafetida
Mango powder
Anardana
Arthritis diet
Aniseed

B
Basil
Bread pizza
Beans soup
Balanced diet
Beverages

C
Carbohydrates
Condiments
Coriander
Cumin
Cinnamon
Clove
Dips
Calcium

Cabbage soup
Coffee
Condurango
Comments

D
Diet
Diarrhoea

F
Fibre
Flax seeds
Fruits facts about
Facts about, nutrition

G
Gastric diet
Ginger pickle

H
Hypertension Diet

I
Iron
Iodine

J
JalCumin

K
Khaata meetha garlic
Kurkure salad

L
Lady finger
Lassi
Lacha tokri

M
Mocktail
Minerals
Minty fruit chart
Mugwort
Mustard

N
Nutty mutty ginger
Nutmeg

O
Oregano

P
Peppermint

Phosphorus
Proteins
Principles of cooking

R
Renal diet
Roughage
Respiratory diet

S
Saffron
Soups
Spaghetti Soup
Shan-E Bread
Shahi Korma
Spices
Sweet dishes
Soups
Snacks

T
Thandai
Tomato Curry
Tamarind
Turmeric
Thyme